A MOTHER'S
WHITE LIE

Jennifer Lipford Petticolas

McClure Publishing, Inc.

Copyright © 2024 by Jennifer Lipford Petticolas

McClure Publishing, Inc.

All rights reserved. Printed and bound in the United States of America. According to the 1976 United States Copyright Act, no portion of this book may be reproduced or utilized in any form or by any means, electronic or mechanical, including photocopying, recording, or by any information storage or retrieval system, except by a reviewer who may quote brief passages in a review to be printed in a magazine or newspaper, without permission in writing from the Publisher or author: Inquiries should be addressed to McClure Publishing, Inc. Permissions Department, 398 West Army Trail Road, Bloomingdale, IL 60108. First Printing: September 28, 2024.

ISBN-13: 979-8-9907047-0-1

Cover Design by Autumn B. Canady

To order additional copies, please contact:

McClure Publishing, Inc.
https://McClurePublishing.com
800-659-4908

~ or ~

Jennifer Lipford Petticolas
Jlp7139@yahoo.com

*In honor of my mother, Clytie Rosser Lipford.
I am who I am because of the sacrifices she made.
My daughters, Kisha and Tameka, and
my grandson, Joshua,
you are my heartbeats.*

WHEREAS some doubts have arisen whether children got by any Englishman upon a negro woman should be slave or ffree, Be it therefore enacted and declared by this present grand assembly, that all children borne in this country shalbe held bond or free only according to the condition of the mother, And that if any christian shall committ ffornication with a negro man or woman, hee or shee soe offending shall pay double the ffines imposed by the former act.

Laws of Virginia, 1662 Act Xll

Every person in whom there is ascertainable any Negro blood shall be deemed and taken to be a colored person, and every person not a colored person not a colored person having one-fourth or more of American Indian blood shall be deemed an American Indian; except that members of Indian tribes existing in this Commonwealth having one-fourth or more of Indian blood less than one-sixteenth of Negro blood shall be deemed tribal Indians.

(Code 1887, § 49; 1910, p. 581.)

A Mother's White Lie

CHAPTER ONE

Sarah

March 2003. The telephone's incessant ringing broke the silence of the early morning, and Sarah Franklin couldn't help but feel a sense of annoyance as she answered. "Hello?" She asked curtly, only to be met with the voice of Mrs. Jefferson, the director at Greener Pastures, requesting her presence at the facility. Feeling a bit embarrassed because of the tone of her greeting, Sarah meekly responded, "Yes, Ma'am. I'll be right there." Sarah looked at the clock. It was seven-thirty. Her hopes for a quiet Saturday morning vanished like vapor in the air. She jumped out of bed and ran to the bathroom to brush her teeth. Looking in the mirror, she scolded herself. *Why didn't I ask* her what was wrong? This is my fault. I saw the signs. But I didn't want to believe ... Daddy is dead. My brother is.... I don't know where. I had finally found love. The voice in her head yelled *Stop! Focus! This is NOT about you!* Reaching for a washcloth, she wiped her face; she did not take the time to shower because there was a sound of urgency in Mrs. Jefferson's voice. There was no time for make-up. Sarah took off her nightshirt, snatched a yellow tee shirt laying on the back of the chair in her bedroom, slid it over her head, slipped on a pair of blue jeans and black flat shoes, grabbed her pocketbook, and was out the door. As she stepped onto her front porch, the fragrances of Sweet Peas and Snap Dragons, planted on opposite sides, stopped her in her tracks and enshrouded her in their aromas. Sarah had always liked the intermingling fragrances, but this morning the scents seemed to be battling one another and were holding her hostage. Her inner voice rang out, commanding her to move. Surveying her surroundings, she exited the front gate and got into her car.

Upon reaching Greener Pastures, Sarah pulled into a parking space and turned off her car. Without even thinking, she opened her car door and started running for the front door of Greener Pastures. Reaching for the door handle, she froze because she could see her reflection in the glass; she still had her night scarf tied around her head. She took a few anxious breaths, then she took one deep breath and released it slowly. *I can't worry about a scarf on my head now! Focus, Sarah, focus! Life changes in the blink of an eye.* She thought. *I thought I could start concentrating on my life or maybe finding my brother. Instead, I am running to Greener Pastures with a scarf tied around my head.*

Rather than checking in with the director, Sarah went straight to room 314, her mother's room. Rose sat in a chair by the window with her hands in her lap. Observing her mother, she thought, *she looks alright*. Entering the room, Sarah called out, "Hey, Mom! How are you doing?" Rose didn't move. She sat motionless with her head bowed. Sarah hesitated for a moment. She felt a knot in the bottom of her stomach. *She must be sleeping. If she were dead, they wouldn't leave her sitting in the chair like that, would they?* "Mom, are you alright?" Rose's hand twitched. Sarah exhaled. *She's alive!* Sarah sat on the edge of the bed near her mother's chair. "Do you want me to brush your hair?" Rose didn't respond. But that wasn't unusual. "Mom, I got a call from Mrs. Jefferson. Have you been eating? I'm sorry I haven't been here in the last two days. I was trying to get some things done in the house. Don't worry. I didn't change a thing in your room or Robert's." Looking around for Rose's hairbrush, Sarah spotted it on the night table on the other side of the bed. Stretching out across the bed, she grabbed the brush and sat up. Rose slowly lifted her head. Sarah gasped; her eyes widened; the brush fell from her hand to the floor. Her mother's face was sallow. Her eyes had dark circles under them. Sarah picked up the hairbrush and placed it on the bed. "Mom! Mom! What happened?" Flustered by her mother's appearance, "Mom, what…. Never mind!" Trying to gather her thoughts, "Why am I asking you? I need some answers. I'll be right back."

Sarah walked briskly to the nurse's station. There was no one there. As Sarah turned to go back to check on her mother, she was face to face with Faye, the hall monitor. *Where the hell did she come from?* Sarah did not want to be bothered by Faye. She thought if she smiled and spoke maybe Faye would go away, so she greeted her with a forced smile. "Hi, Faye, do you know where I can find the nurse?"

Just as Faye pointed to the staff restroom, a short chubby blonde woman opened the door. Sarah asked, "Are you the nurse on duty?"

Patting her hair and adjusting her blouse, the chubby blonde woman jumped when Sarah spoke. "Oh, my goodness! You startled me! I didn't realize you were standing there. Yes, ma'am, I'm the duty nurse. Do you need something?"

Sarah tried to remain calm, "Yes, I do need something. I need some answers."

With a cheery accommodating smile, the nurse responded, "Hopefully, I can provide you with the answers you are seeking."

"I'm Sarah, Rose's daughter. My mother is in room 314. Can you tell me what happened to her?"

"Oh yes, the director is expecting you. Let me call her." The nurse turned her back to Sarah and picked up the telephone. "Hi, Mrs. Jefferson, Rose's daughter is here. Okay. I will. Thank you. Bye!" Turning to Sarah, she smiled and said, "She is on her way up. Why don't you go to your mother's room, and I will let her know where you are."

"Thank you!"

As Sarah turned to walk back to her mother's room, the elevator door opened. Mrs. Jefferson stepped out of the elevator and called out. "Miss Franklin."

Sarah pivoted and responded, "Yes."

Mrs. Emily Jefferson, a short woman with legs that resembled tree trunks, smiled at Sarah. She professionally conveyed her appreciation saying, "Thank you for coming so quickly."

"Yes, ma'am. What happened to my mom? She was fine two days ago. Well as fine, in her condition, as can be expected."

Mrs. Jefferson pointed to a bench against the wall in the corridor, "Let's sit over here."

Sarah could feel her insides trembling. Trying to control her voice, she swallowed and responded, "If you don't mind, I would prefer to go to my mother's room. She didn't look well."

She could see and hear Sarah's fear. Trying to reassure Sarah with a little smile, she said, "I know. I didn't think she would take it this hard."

Sarah needed clarification. "Take what this hard?"

As they made their way down the hallway to Rose's room, Mrs. Jefferson couldn't help but giggle inwardly. How would she explain Rose's condition? She reached out, touching Sarah's arm gently. "She's missing Sidney," she revealed.

Stunned, Sarah stopped one door from her mother's room. She grabbed Mrs. Jefferson's arm. "Oh, my goodness, no! When did he die?"

"No, no, dear!" Mrs. Jefferson responded with a smile. "Sidney didn't die. Donald moved him to another facility." Mrs. Jefferson gently touched Sarah's arm. She tried to reassure her. "Give your mother a little time and she will adjust, but I wanted you to know she wasn't sleeping or eating. I thought maybe you could help us in coaxing her to eat."

Confused, "Why? Donald seemed happy about his father's care here at Greener Pastures."

"He was."

"Then I don't understand. Why did Donald move his father to another nursing home?"

Mrs. Jefferson scratched the back of her head. She was trying not to blush, but she felt her cheeks getting warm, "Well, Sarah, Donald walked in on his father and your mother naked. They were in bed together having sex."

Sarah gasped and lowered her head. "They were what?" The question was rhetorical. She didn't want Mrs. Jefferson to repeat it. Embarrassed, her heart sank. It was hard to picture these two old bodies having any sexual desires. She had not known her mother being with any man other than her father. Then Sarah thought, *Aah, Daddy! That makes sense.* Embarrassment caused words to stick in her throat. Covering a cough, she turned to Mrs. Jefferson, "I am so sorry this happened. I don't know what to say."

Mrs. Jefferson could see Sarah was embarrassed, but also concerned about her mother. She smiled and asked, "May I make a suggestion?"

"Yes, please."

"Would you consider putting your mother in a semi-private room? I think having someone in the room with her might help bring her out of this depression."

A feeling of guilt washed over Sarah. This might not have happened if she had done as her mother had requested. "A roommate. Yes, that would be great."

"Good! We will move her to room 245 tomorrow on the second floor."

CHAPTER TWO

Greener Pastures

A Saturday in August 2003. Death before death wrapped his arms around bodies, minds, and souls: stealing memories, stripping away dignity, and causing pain for everyone he touched. The pleasure his victims could find during their darkness was taken away by the living who claimed they cared.

It was almost time. Janie Ruth, a spunky woman of seventy-five, hobbled past Karen Bush, who sat in her wheelchair outside of her door. Her contralto voice singing, "Precious Lord, take my hand. Lead me on. Let me stand. I am tired. I am weak. I am worn," reverberated through the hall and took rest in the spirits of those listening.

Faye Jones, the self-appointed residential hall monitor, once walked these halls as a nurse; but now she was a resident. With her hands behind her back like a soldier, Faye confronted anyone she didn't know, asking, "What's going on here?"

As Janie Ruth walked past, Faye turned on her heels with her hands still behind her back and watched Janie Ruth walk down the hallway. Fred Minor rolled his wheelchair past Janie Ruth, chanting in a raspy adenoidal voice, "Hey honey, hey honey."

Janie Ruth smiled, thinking; *He always sounds like he has a flock of geese stuck in his nostrils.* Moving down the corridor with the support of her cane, Janie Ruth looked in the rooms to her right and left. She saw a husband wiping the drool from his wife's mouth in one room. Several rooms down the corridor, she saw a granddaughter lovingly combing her grandmother's hair. Televisions blasted.

Visitors buzzed around like a swarm of bees in many of the rooms. In a few rooms, preachers prayed like every tomorrow would be covered in darkness. But other rooms were empty of activity except for rising and falling chests of once vibrant people – now empty shells.

As she walked looking in rooms, memories of Melissa, her previous roommate came to mind. Melissa, who had diabetes with acute kidney problems, was her third roommate. When she took her last breath, a nurse asked Janie Ruth to leave the room while Melissa's family had their final moments with her body and said their goodbyes.

On Rose Franklin's first day in the nursing home, Janie Ruth was a part of the welcoming committee. Upon her arrival, Rose's daughter, Sarah, had requested that her mother be put in a private room, but after the incident with Sidney, she withdrew that request. Janie Ruth remembered looking at Rose on that first day, trying to come up with a word to describe her: Regal. She was regal. Every strand of hair on her head was in place. Her crisp white blouse was neatly tucked into a charcoal grey skirt. Janie

Ruth was excited when she was told Rose would be her roommate.

Janie Ruth slowed her pace a bit as she approached her own room. She saw Rose sitting on her bed, staring at the open door. *Should I walk past, or should I stop? Maybe I shouldn't stay out of the room so much, but I hate seeing her like this. No, I can't just walk past. I need to keep trying. Who knows, maybe I'll see a glimmer of the old Rose.*

After a slight hesitation, she turned and hobbled to the opened door. There, sat Rose, as still as a statue, slouched on the edge of the bed. Her feeble shoulders looked as if they supported the weight of the world. Her breathing was barely visible, and she stared as though she was in a hypnotic trance. Janie Ruth stood there a moment before she spoke.

"Rose, are you alright? Please don't be sad." Rose didn't say a word. Janie Ruth sighed and leaned against the frame of the door. "Don't let them get you down." Janie Ruth didn't know whether Rose could hear her. After Sidney left, it was as though a dark abyss swallowed Rose, sucking the life from her body, mind, and soul.

Janie Ruth stepped into the room and kept talking like Rose had participated in the conversation. "You can't give up, old girl! If you end up in the hospital, that might mean you'll lose your bed, and I'll have to get used to someone new."

Janie Ruth wasn't aware Rose could afford to be in a private room in a more exclusive facility nor was she aware Rose being in Greener Pastures and having a roommate was Rose's choice.

Janie Ruth turned to walk away but stopped when a sorrowful feeling washed over her. She stood rubbing her forehead like she was trying to conjure up a forgotten thought. Her eyes brimmed with tears, and her brow furrowed softly across her mocha face. For seventy-five, her skin was smooth with no wrinkles. She pulled a tissue from the pocket of her house dress and dabbed her slightly twisted lips. Then she turned back to Rose and uttered, "Listen, I know how you felt about Sidney, but his son is in control. Not you. Not Sarah. Not Sidney." She stopped talking for a moment and stood enveloped in silence. Then she whispered as though she was sharing a secret, "Parents become children, and children become parents. When we get old and disabled, our children don't always care about our happiness the way we cared about theirs. I'll see you later."

As she turned to walk away, a cloud of sadness, like dust, covered Janie Ruth and settled in every crevice of her being. She took a deep breath to shake the feeling. As she exhaled, she wondered if she would ever get used to the competing intermingling smells of old age, urine, disinfectant, and death. *People have children thinking they will have someone who will have their best interest at heart and take care of them when they're old*, Janie Ruth thought. *It's all a joke! Just one big joke!*

She continued her walk toward the community room, the heart of Greener Pastures Nursing Home and Rehabilitation Center. There was life here. Happiness may have eluded other parts of Greener Pastures, but it found a home here. This room was a church on Sundays, a classroom for Bible study on Wednesdays, and a game room for bingo on Saturdays. One end of the room had a sofa, two chairs, a coffee table, and magazines. A fireplace divided the room. The other end of the room was set up for bingo. The evening sun shining through a vast glass window filled the room with warm light.

Janie Ruth stood at the door for a moment before entering. She didn't want to carry into the room the gloom and despair that had seeped into her spirit. Softly patting her salt and pepper afro, she smiled and whispered, "Tonight is my night." She entered the room and looked around. Thinking she would be the first, she was surprised to see someone she didn't know already there.

Even though the man was in a wheelchair, Janie Ruth could tell he was tall. His brownish-gray hair had a bit of curl and was still amazingly thick. He was dressed in khakis and a green Brooks Brothers shirt. His expensive green striped socks and his nursing home-issued slippers looked out of place.

He greeted her with a smile. "Hi, I'm Richard Fallon." Richard extended his hand while remaining in his chair. "Please excuse my hands. They're cold."

Janie Ruth's laughter filled the room, "How would I know? So are mine. I think most of us here have cold hands. We're just one step from the grave."

"I don't believe that. You have a strange sense of humor."

"Believe what you want. Anyway, I'm Janie Ruth Howard. People call me Janie Ruth. I've never seen you here."

"Today is my first day here." Richard leaned forward in his chair. "Excuse me for not getting up."

"Getting up! That's funny! You're in a wheelchair. No one expects you to get up around here." Janie Ruth mumbled under her breath, "White people."

"Are you talking to me?"

"No … yes…. I was just saying welcome to Greener Pastures. What room are you in?"

"I'm in room 205. I'm only here for six weeks."

"Oh, you're rooming with Jessie. Well, however long you're here, I'm in room 245."

Richard looked at her, puzzled. "What do you mean by however long I am here?"

"I didn't mean anything. It's just…."

"It's just what?"

"It's just that I've seen people come in here for rehab thinking they're going home, but their children have different plans for them. Their children decide that coming back home isn't in the best interest of their aging parents."

"I don't have children, but that has to be heartbreaking."

"Lucky you! Yeah … yeah, it is heartbreaking."

Richard watched as Janie Ruth hobbled over to a table containing stacks of bingo cards. Looking back at Richard, she said, "I hope you didn't pick out all the lucky ones."

"I didn't pick out any."

"Why? Aren't you playing?"

"Playing what?"

"Bingo!"

"Bingo? I didn't know bingo was tonight. I am sitting here because I am too tired to roll myself to my room."

"Suit yourself. Tonight is my night. I want to get my cards before anyone can pick over them."

Suddenly, they heard a raspy voice from the hallway, "Cigars, cigarettes, Tiparillos."

Richard frowned and cocked his head to one side as though trying to ensure he heard correctly. "They allow people to sell cigarettes here?"

Janie Ruth knew the room would soon be filled with other residents, so she ignored Richard's question. She busied herself, selecting her bingo cards.

The words "Cigars, cigarettes, Tiparillos" floated in again from outside the room.

Richard's mind started to drift as the words dissipated into the air. He smiled and closed his eyes as he remembered 1960s Tiparillos ads. *'Should a gentleman offer a Tiparillo to a lady?' That ad with the picture of the violinist was hot,* he thought. His smile widened as he conjured up the image of the old ad. *Opened blouse, cleavage, and a violin. 'Maybe tonight she might like it, the slim cigar with a white tip.'* Richard chuckled to himself and thought, *who needed Playboy?*

This time when the words floated into the room, Lillie Megginson followed them. Richard opened his eyes. When he saw her, he stifled his laughter with a fake cough. *She is not a Tiparillo girl. Gravity hasn't been her friend,* he thought.

As Lillie walked past, Richard noticed a cigarette box attached to the walker she used for support. Dressed in a red and black V-necked cigarette girl costume, Lillie's breasts appeared almost nonexistent. They hung like two deflated tires. She wore orthopedic shoes and a cotton support hose attached to a red garter belt.

"Why is she dressed like that? Is she really selling cigarettes?" Richard asked.

"When she was young, she was a cigarette girl and thinks she still is. When her family put her here, they asked the administration to let her wear her cigarette girl costume."

"Why?"

"I'm told they wanted her to hold on to any memories as long as possible."

"That's funny. And they think the costume will stop her memory loss?"

"No, I don't think so, but Lillie's attitude is much better, and she is easier to deal with when she is in that ridiculous outfit." Janie Ruth looked up momentarily to see Lillie was headed in her direction. "Not now, Lillie."

"Sh…sh…she's trying to steal from my cigarette box!" Lillie shouted to Richard.

Looking at Lillie, Janie Ruth rolled her eyes and said, "I don't have time for you right now. No one could touch that tray even if they wanted to. You guard it like it contains gold," Janie Ruth replied. "Go on now. I'm busy!" she continued shuffling through the cards, stopping, and rubbing every other one like she was expecting some electric current to run up her arms, saying it was a winner. With a stack of bingo cards stuffed in her floral house dress pocket, Janie Ruth hobbled to the table where Richard sat. Amused by her, he watched as she took the cards from her pocket and meticulously arranged them on the table. She then placed her chips above each card.

"I don't understand what's so exciting about the game. There is no real challenge." Richard said.

Janie Ruth looked at him through squinted eyes. *Privileged prick! Old age hasn't kicked his ass yet.* She gave him a fake smile, "Maybe not for you, but for many of us, it's a challenge to just get here to this room. It can be challenging for some of us to pick up this small chip and move it from one place to another."

"I'm sorry. I guess I was being a bit insensitive."

"Yes, I'd say you were. For me, bingo was Santa Claus."

"Santa Claus? What do you mean?"

"You don't look like you've ever lacked for anything. I bet you've never missed a meal or was ever scared there would be no presents under the tree on Christmas morning."

Richard smiled and thought *you're right*, but responded, "Looks can be very deceiving."

"When I was about ten years old, my mama lost her job. She didn't have money to give my brothers, sisters, and me Christmas. She acted like she was angry at the world. She'd yell at us for the least little thing. We were kids; we didn't know what was going on. Her best friend, Peggy, told her she needed a girls' night out, so she paid my mama's way into a bingo game. I don't know if it was luck or God, but my mama won the last game of the night – the black-out game."

"Maybe they're the same."

"What?"

"Luck and God."

Janie Ruth gave him a dismissive shoulder shrug. "Could be. Anyway, Mama won five hundred dollars. We had the best Christmas ever. Peggy came over on Christmas day to help us celebrate. I remember my mama hugging her. She never said anything; she just held on to Peggy and cried."

Janie Ruth felt tears welling up in her eyes. "Look, you're here, so you might as well play."

A woman's tears made Richard feel inadequate. He remembered his mother crying when he was a young boy, and he could do nothing to console her. He wanted to reach out to comfort Janie Ruth, but he did not know her so he said, "Janie Ruth, it will be my pleasure." Richard leaned over to push his wheelchair forward.

"Stay put. I'll get the cards for you."

"I will only need one."

Janie Ruth hobbled over to the table and back. She pulled three cards and some chips from her pocket and gave them to Richard.

"Thank you."

A crescendo of voices came from the corridor, accompanied by a symphony of feet shuffling, bedroom slippers flip-flopping, wheelchairs rattling, canes stumping, and walkers plopping. Janie Ruth looked at Richard and said, "Here they come."

Denise, Brittney, Bessie, and Ned entered the room. Lillie greeted them with "Cigars, cigarettes, Tiparillos."

"Lillie must be having a good day; she has on make-up," said Bessie.

Denise and Brittney nodded their heads in agreement. Lillie's gray hair was in two braids and bobby-pinned on top of her head. At eighty-one, she looked every minute of her age and then some. The wrinkles around her mouth and eyes were from years of smoking. Lillie tried to hide the deep creases in her caramel-colored skin with make-up on her good days. On her bad days, she forgot she even had a face.

Ned was already at the table selecting his cards.

"I need some help," Bessie whined. "This is my first time playing bingo."

"Oh, so you're a virgin," Ned chuckled.

"Lord, no! I have three children." Winking her eye at Ned, Bessie laughed and said, "I've had my share of men in my day."

"I mean a bingo virgin," said Ned. "Your bingo cherry will be popped here tonight at Greener Pastures."

"Oh my! I'm excited. Imagine me, at my age, being deflowered. I feel all tingly."

Ned laughed, "I hope it's good for you."

"I'm getting a bit warm and flustered," said Bessie.

"For crying out loud! It's a bingo game! Not a roll in the hay!" exclaimed Denise.

Bessie giggled like an adolescent, "What's your problem, Denise? Don't be a blocker. At our age, we get our jollies when and however we can."

Denise responded begrudgingly. "Look at me! How can I block anything?"

The room started to fill with other residents and aides. George Freeman and Emily Wilson, octogenarian friends of Janie Ruth, entered: Emily, frail and hunched over; George pushed in a wheelchair. They selected bingo cards and joined Janie Ruth and Richard at their table.

"George and Emily, this is Richard. He just got here today," said Janie Ruth.

Emily smiled and nodded her head.

She looks like a hunched-over bobblehead, Richard thought. Richard smiled back. "So glad to meet you. How are you this evening?"

Emily said nothing. She just continued to nod.

On the other hand, George looked down at his legs and then up at Richard. George then moved his ebony arthritic hands up and down both legs and spoke. "I've had a hip replacement. I have two new knees. I've had two bypass surgeries. I've had prostate cancer. My diabetes is out of control. At times I can hardly feel my hands and feet. I have arthritis. I'm taking forty-three different medicines. I get dizzy sometimes. Other than that, I feel fine. How're you?" George asked.

After listening to George's list of ailments, Richard responded, "I'm doing fine!"

"George, you don't have a monopoly on getting old," Janie Ruth snapped.

The crackle of a microphone sliced through the sea of aged voices. A young man in a plaid jacket, accompanied by a nurse's aide, stood in front of the residents. He looked over the group and said, "You're looking good out there this evening! Are you ready to play?" Mumbling voices bounced off the walls as the bingo caller filled the basket with the numbered balls. Nodding his head towards his right, he said, "This is Penelope. She's here in case anyone gets too excited and might need help. Everything seems in place, so let's start this game." He turned the basket handle once and stopped, "I forgot to remind you don't clear your card when someone calls bingo. Penelope will assist with checking to make sure we really have a winner. Tonight, we'll start with the straight pattern. Now let's play BINGO! Eyes on your cards!" Once again, he turned the handle. The numbered glass balls rattled and fell one by one in the slot beneath the basket.

Although he called each number slowly, loudly, and precisely, Emily yelled out after each call, "What did he say?" Her frail voice echoed through the room.

Janie Ruth and George ignored Emily. Richard looked around the room, amazed at the intense concentration of the players.

Janie Ruth stared at her cards like a cat about to sneak up on a bird. She waved her hands over them like a minister about to lay hands on a sinner.

After the fifth call, Brittney yelled, "Janie Ruth, shut Emily up so we can hear the damn numbers!"

Never looking up, Janie Ruth reached over, touched Emily, and said, "Emily, turn on your hearing aid."

Emily yelled, "What? What did you say?"

The room became a mass of verbal confusion. The bingo caller stopped calling numbers and asked, "Did someone yell bingo?"

Lillie stood up, leaned on her walker, and repeatedly said, "Cigars, cigarettes, Tiparillos."

Janie Ruth yelled, "My God! Emily, turn on your hearing aid!"

"He's going too fast! I didn't hear what he said," Emily yelled.

Janie Ruth continued to study her cards as she spoke, "George, tonight is my night. I can't deal with her right now!"

George patted Emily's feeble white hand covered with brown age spots, "She needs a new battery for her hearing aid." He looked into her eyes and yelled, "Emily, I'll put the dots on your card for you." He reached over and took her card.

With sadness in her drooping blue eyes, Emily looked at George and said, "But I want to play."

Brittney showed no compassion. "Shut her up so we can play."

A brief hush fell over the room. The bingo caller intruded on the silence with, "Let's keep this game going. The next number is B-12."

As the game progressed, excitement once again filled the room. Richard decided watching the residents was more amusing than placing chips on his card. *Damn! I see nothing but the top of gray and balding heads. They take this bingo game seriously. This is funny!* Richard chuckled to himself. *Everybody waiting and listening for their winning number. No, this is not funny! This is life!* A dull pain eased up Richard's right leg. Tiredness washed over him. *Yeah, this is life. It doesn't matter whether you wait it out patiently or feel stressed and anxious; it doesn't matter! It doesn't matter! In time everyone's number will come up.*

Massaging his leg, Richard heard mumbling from every corner of the room.

One person uttered, "N-40, come on, N-40."

Someone else pleaded, "I-33, I-33."

Janie Ruth waved her hands over her cards, begging in a whisper, "Okay now, G-22, O-14, B-4, N-25. Come on now. Make me a winner."

She had four cards. All she needed was one number to be a winner. She knew luck was on her side. At the very moment, she allowed a smile to radiate across her face; she heard Denise yell bingo.

Groans and curse words floated through the air. The caller stood with a silly grin and asked, "Did I just hear someone say the magic word?"

"Bingo!" Denise shouted again with all the enthusiasm her frail frame could muster.

"Well, hold on, young lady. Penelope will be there in two shakes of a lamb's tail to check your card."

With a wry smile on her face, Denise looked around the room. She thought, *Look at me. I'm a winner. Just seven months ago, before New Year's Day, if I had won anything, I would've been on my feet doing a modified jitterbug happy dance. I'll never dance again. That asshole of a truck driver made sure of that when he decided texting his girlfriend was more important than paying attention to the road. In the hospital for three months. I can't even sit up straight. My back is curved. I can't....*

Penelope, an emaciated-looking redhead with freckles. stood looking down at Denise. "Let me see your card."

Denise removed her gnarled, arthritic hands from her card so Penelope could check it.

Someone coughing and another passing gas were the only sounds heard. Penelope declared that it was a good win. The caller instructed everyone to clear their cards and take a fifteen-minute break.

Lillie stood up with the support of her walker and made her way over to Denise, "Cigars, cigarettes, Tiparillos."

Denise reached into Lillie's cigarette box with both hands for a prize. She pulled out a pair of fuzzy socks.

Bessie looked at Ned, smiling, "Well, I didn't win this first game, Ned, but my bingo cherry has been popped."

Ned teasingly asked, "Did it feel good to you, ole girl?"

"It was a bit painful in the beginning because of Emily." Bessie stood up. Her silver hair fell out of its bun as she tossed her head to the side. She took a deep breath and said, "But towards the end, I enjoyed it."

Denise watched Bessie with more jealousy than disgust because she wanted to feel beautiful and flirty. She was only fifty-five, younger than Bessie. Greener Pastures was her permanent home because she couldn't care for herself and had no family to care for her. Anger slowly seethed from the pit of her stomach; she needed to speak before it erupted. "Bessie, you need to sit your eighty-three-year-old behind down somewhere."

Brittney defended Bessie, "Why does she need to do that? Denise, why can't you be happy? You just won the first game."

"She is too old to act like a fool," Denise said flatly.

With her hands on her hips, Bessie looked at Denise and asked, "Who says I'm too old? What about Rose and Sidney? Rose is eighty-nine, and Sidney is ninety-five."

Denise laughed and shook her head. "Yeah, Rose and Sidney! That's a painful joke."

Richard looked at Janie Ruth and asked, "Who are Rose and Sidney?"

The microphone sputtered to life, "Get back to your seats and get your cards ready. Time to start another bingo game!"

CHAPTER THREE

Greener Pastures

A friendship had blossomed between Janie Ruth and Richard, making his daily visits to her a cherished routine. Today, Richard felt unsettled by her absence throughout the morning. "She's likely in the community room," he surmised. Upon entering, he noticed Karen positioned in her wheelchair beside the expansive glass window, her head angled towards the sunlight, eyes shut, humming a melody that tugged at Richard's recognition. He paused to listen, attempting to place the tune, yet it eluded his immediate recollection.

Upon surveying the room, he noticed some residents idly gazing at one another. Others sat with their eyes fixated on the door, reminiscent of children eagerly awaiting the arrival of Santa

Claus. She wasn't there. On the way to his room, he decided to stop by Janie Ruth's room. When he got to the door, he saw Rose sitting on the edge of her bed. Her breakfast tray sat on the table in front of her. She was fiddling with her napkin. She picked it up, folded it, placed it on her tray, and gave it a little pat. She did this several times. Then she picked up something and attempted to eat eggs. The wrinkled lines around her eyes, the dark circles, and the bags beneath them made her look tired and frail. He sat in his wheelchair for a moment watching her. He choked back tears. His heart ached. He wanted to say something but decided against it. As he started wheeling his chair away from the door, Janie Ruth stepped out of the bathroom.

"Looking for me?"

Robert cleared his throat, "Yes, I just wanted to speak."

Janie Ruth stood with her hands on her hips. "Well?"

He looked puzzled. "Well, what?"

Janie Ruth giggled. "Speak! You said you wanted to speak."

Richard laughed. "Good morning, Janie Ruth?"

"Good morning, Richard Fallon. How are you?"

"I am well. I just left physical therapy." Richard nodded toward Rose. "Your roommate?"

"Yes, Rose Franklin."

He sat for a moment watching Rose. Then he asked, "Why is she eating with those?"

Janie Ruth arched her eyebrows, cocked her head to one side, and inquired, "What would you do with them?"

"Come on Janie Ruth, you know what I mean."

Throwing her head back and letting out a boisterous laugh, "Well, this morning when the nurse came in, Rose had someone's dentures on her breakfast tray. The nurse and I watched Rose pick them up. We had no idea where she got them, but we watched as she examined them and put them back on her tray. The nurse pointed to Rose's mouth and explained to Rose that you use them to eat with. I guess Rose thought they were her eating utensils because she started scooping up her eggs and putting them in her mouth. We got a good chuckle watching her. The nurse was just happy that she was eating. She told me she was going to see if anyone had reported their dentures missing. Until then, they belong to Rose."

To rid himself of the sad feeling that was trying to wash over him, he chuckled, "Whatever it takes. Does she have children?"

"Twins. A daughter and son. I've never met her son, but her daughter visits almost every day. I've only known for her to miss maybe two days since Rose has been here."

A Mother's White Lie

CHAPTER FOUR

Greener Pastures

In Greener Pastures, Richard had expected to find death walking the corridors keeping watch in rooms of souls he was waiting to claim, and creeping unexpectedly out of crevices claiming souls who thought tomorrows were theirs. He had expected enormous sadness, but instead, he realized he was waking up in the mornings smiling and looking forward to seeing Janie Ruth. As he entered the community room, he saw Rose with a nurse's aide trying to coax her to eat something.

"Rose, are you going to eat something today?"

Rose stared at the floor. She whispered, "Charlie is coming."

"Rose, you didn't eat supper yesterday. You have to eat something today," the nurse's aide said firmly,

Rose screamed, "Charlie!"

A bit agitated, the nurse's aide said, "Sidney is not coming, Rose! Now eat something."

At the end of the bingo game, Richard remembered hearing Denise say, *Yeah, Rose and Sidney! That's a painful joke.* He wondered *why they were saying Sidney when she was asking for Charlie. Who is Sidney, and what was the joke?* Richard sat at a card table with a checkerboard on it. He fiddled with the checker pieces but positioned himself to hear what Rose said to the nurse's aide.

"Charlie is coming to see me today."

The aide responded, "Rose, his name is Sidney, not Charlie, and he will not be coming to see you today!"

Richard thought the nurse's aide was being a bit harsh. He wondered about Sidney. *Why wouldn't he come to see her?*

Rose picked up a magazine. She turned it over and flipped through it.

"What should I do with this?" Rose asked, but before the nurse's aide could reply, she started to chant in a whining tone, "Charlie is coming today. Charlie is coming today."

The nurse's aide was visibly frustrated. "Rose, listen to me! Sidney is not coming today."

Rose seemed oblivious to what was being said to her. She continued flipping through the magazine.

"Do you want me to read the magazine to you?"

Rose opened the magazine and placed it on her head.

The nurse's aide reached for the magazine. "No, Rose. Don't put that on your head. It's a magazine, not a hat."

Richard observed the exchange between Rose and the nurse's aide, taking in every nuance. The dynamics unfolding between them did not escape his notice. As her frustration mounted, Rose started to take off her shoes.

In a raised voice, the nurse's aide exclaimed, "Stop, Rose!" She snatched the shoe from Rose's hand just as she put it on her head.

Richard was wrestling with the decision to intervene. Just as he mustered the courage to suggest she be more patient and her tone more compassionate, he felt a hand on his shoulder. It was Janie Ruth.

"Hey, Richard, we've got to stop meeting like this!" They both laughed.

Richard slowly pulled himself up, "Have a seat, Janie Ruth."

Janie Ruth smiled. "Always a gentleman." Balancing herself with the help of her cane, she did a little curtsey, "Don't mind if I do. How are you today?"

"Good, very good! I hope I will not have to be here for six weeks."

"Oh, so you don't like my company anymore?"

"No, no! You know that's not it."

"I know. I've been meaning to ask why you came here for rehab? I imagine you in a swankier place."

"Looking for greener pastures, I guess." He laughed. "Janie Ruth, how has it been for you here?" Richard stacked the checker pieces on the table.

"Okay. The nurses and the aides here are great. I have no real complaints. My daughter lives in Texas. She is a rep for a pharmaceutical company. She put me here after my second stroke. I had paralysis on one side. They have taken really good care of me here."

Richard was surprised to learn Janie Ruth had a child. "You have a daughter? You've never mentioned her before."

"Really? I see you have the checkerboard out. Were you looking for someone to play a game of checkers with you?"

"I get it. You don't want to talk about your daughter. The board was here when I got here, but I'd love to play. I haven't played checkers since I was in high school."

"So, you're ready for a butt whipping!" exclaimed Janie Ruth.

"We'll see about that. Let's just set this board up and see who says King Me the most."

Janie Ruth declared, "I'm red."

"Okay, I guess that means I'm black."

"Now, that is funny." Janie Ruth laughed.

They set up the checkerboard and started to play. Janie Ruth studied the board.

"Janie Ruth, you're looking at that board the same way you look at those bingo cards."

"Yes. Games are like life. You don't want to make the wrong move if you can help it."

They both studied the board after each move.

"It's your move." Janie Ruth said, smiling.

"I know." He reached out to make a move, but he changed his mind. There was no way Richard wanted Janie Ruth to beat him.

Janie Ruth laughed. "Wake me up when you make your move."

"Funny." Richard made a move but quickly realized it was what Janie Ruth was waiting for. He thought, *how could I have been so stupid? She set up a trap, and I walked right into it.* He reached out to move the piece back.

"Not a chance." She made a double jump and said, "King me!"

"Don't gloat," he said.

"I can't help myself. Now, tell me something. How did you manage to break your hip?"

"Are you trying to distract me?" Richard asked.

Sticking her chest out, Janie Ruth said, "No, I don't need to distract you. This is my game."

"I hate to admit it, but I think you're right." He studied the board but saw nothing. "I fell down some stairs while I…." Richard stopped talking when he heard Rose. He looked over at Rose and saw her take her shoe off again. She then tried to put the magazine on her foot.

"I've got to get ready," Rose explained.

"No, Rose, put your shoe back on. Here, let me help you." After a bit of a struggle, the nurse's aide took the magazine from Rose.

Rose looked at her and said, "Charlie."

"Who is Charlie?" The nurse's aide asked.

"Sarah, you know Charlie."

"Rose, I'm not your daughter Sarah."

Agitated and tearful she asked, "Why are you saying that?" Striking at the aide and yelling in a high-pitched shrill, "You are being mean! You are Sarah!"

Richard's body stiffened. He cocked his head to the side as he listened. Janie Ruth looked across the table at him. His face had become a veil of sadness. She tapped on the table.

"Richard, it's your move."

For a moment, Richard appeared to be in a trance. Janie Ruth tapped on the table a second time.

"Richard, is there something wrong?"

"I was just watching the nurse's aide with your roommate. It's so sad. Who are Sidney and Charlie?"

Janie Ruth nodded in agreement. "Yes, it is sad, but it is what life is for some of us."

A somber cloud shrouded his spirit. He recognized the profound sorrow he had anticipated upon arriving at Greener Pastures was a constant companion for Janie Ruth and the other residents. Contemplating his own future, he unintentionally asked aloud, "I wonder what will happen to me when I'm old?"

Janie Ruth laughed. "What do you mean when you are old? You're no spring chicken."

"I know, but do you understand what I'm saying?"

"I do."

"Who are Sidney and Charlie?"

Janie Ruth shook her head, "Another sad story. I'll tell you, but not now."

Disappointed, Richard said, "I think the nurse's aide is a bit harsh with her."

"She isn't. She is very patient with Rose, but she can be a bit difficult. It's not Rose but the Alzheimer's."

"Maybe you're right, but can't she just play along? Telling her that she isn't her daughter will not make her recognize her daughter, will it?"

"Richard, I don't know. Besides, it's not my concern. Just know Rose isn't being mistreated. I am ready to whip you again."

Richard was not completely satisfied, but he stopped talking. He studied the board. As he was about to move, he asked, "Janie Ruth, how do you know she is not being mistreated?"

"Richard, I told you her daughter is here almost daily to check on her."

"You did. That's good." Just as Richard started to study the board again, the words cigars, cigarettes, and Tiparillos floated through the air.

CHAPTER FIVE

Greener Pastures

They had no connection, but they occupied the same space at the same time; they shared the same fear. As the nurse's aide assisted Rose from her chair and guided her towards the community room door, Janie Ruth noticed Richard's intense focus on what was happening. He was so engrossed in watching Rose that he failed to notice Lillie had entered the room and stood before him. Lillie slowly moved her walker forward, causing the table to shift slightly and startling Richard, who then focused his attention on her. To his surprise, Richard felt a sense of joy and contentment upon seeing Lillie, giving him a legitimate reason to smile. Janie Ruth slid her chair back from the table to prevent it from hitting her in her chest.

"Lillie, what's the matter with you?" Janie Ruth asked.

"Cigars, cigarettes, Tiparillos."

Janie Ruth stared at Lillie. "If you keep pushing this table, I'm going to make you look like some cigars, cigarettes, Tiparillos."

Richard jumped up to pull out a chair for Lillie to sit. "Janie Ruth, don't be like that."

Looking bewildered, Lillie looked from Richard to the chair he was standing behind, waiting for her to sit. "It's time for a change," Lillie said.

Not knowing what to do or say, Richard nodded in agreement. He heard Lillie talking, but he was still thinking about Rose. His thoughts were interrupted when he felt a hand on his hand.

Lillie moved beside the chair Richard was still standing behind. "Should a gentleman offer a lady a Tiparillo?"

Startled by what Lillie just asked, Richard said, "Excuse me."

Janie Ruth looked at Richard, patted his hand, and smiled. She was used to Lillie. She chuckled, "Richard, sit down. Lillie will sit down when she is ready. She is a walking commercial."

"It's what's up front that counts," chanted Lillie.

Janie Ruth was trying hard not to laugh. "Lillie, do you remember Richard? He was at the bingo game."

Lillie responded, "Blow in her face, and she will follow you anywhere."

Richard settled into his seat, a smile playing on his lips as he observed Lillie. Her reactions suggested a contentment that seemed to pierce through the veil of her dementia. Meanwhile, memories of Rose began to resurface, casting a shadow over his mood. She appeared so isolated and desolate. He found himself wishing that Rose could find a sanctuary of joy within the shadows of her mind.

Bringing his attention back to Janie Ruth and Lillie, Richard said, "I feel like I'm in a 1950s/1960s cigarette ad."

"Lillie worked as a cigarette girl," said Janie Ruth.

"I remember you telling me that at the bingo game."

"She was a cigarette girl at the Club Harlem in the 1960s and early 70s."

Excitedly, he asked, "Club Harlem in Atlantic City?"

Janie Ruth asked, "Yes, you know it?"

"I lived in New York."

"Really? What brought you to Virginia?"

Richard hesitated before responding, "Retirement."

Janie Ruth tapped the chair, inviting Lillie to sit, but Lillie paid no attention. Janie Ruth was thrilled; this was her chance to discover something about Richard. Whenever she inquired about his life, he deftly shifted the conversation. But now, there would be no avoiding it. "What did you do in New York?" Janie Ruth asked.

He wanted to say it was none of her business, but he had a fondness for Janie Ruth. Perhaps this was his opportunity for redemption. Weighed down by a truth that yearned for release, he remembered the old saying that confession is good for the soul. Richard did not share his life, a trait he shared with Janie Ruth. He wasn't prepared for an inquisition from her or anyone else. Pausing, he collected his thoughts before answering her question. "I worked for a newspaper. I saw Cab Calloway, Ella Fitzgerald, Nina Simone, Sam Cooke, Sammy Davis, Jr., and Billy Paul there."

"What? You saw all those people at your job at the newspaper?"

"No, Janie Ruth, at Club Harlem."

"What? Janie Ruth was surprised. "I've never been to New York or New Jersey, but what I've heard of Club Harlem from

Lillie during her clear-headed times, I thought it was a Black club."

Even though he liked Janie Ruth, he wanted to respond to her with *who cares what you thought?* But maybe this was his moment to start his spiritual healing. He realized he couldn't keep running away from the truth because whenever he looked over his shoulder, he saw himself running, trying to catch himself. He had fabricated a truth that had brought him much success but had pierced a hole so deep in his heart he often felt his soul had escaped his body. More times than not, he felt like an empty shell. He looked Janie Ruth directly in her eyes and said, "In fact, I was there on Easter Sunday in 1972, when Tyrone "Fat" Palmer was gunned down."

Lillie chimed in with another line from a Tiparillo ad, "You've come a long way, baby."

They both laughed at Lillie.

"She might not understand what she is saying," Richard said, "but she is right. Life has a way of bringing you a long way and then dumping on you."

Janie Ruth and Richard stared at one another as though they were looking at their own reflections in a mirror. Gazing at Richard, Janie Ruth saw something she hadn't detected before. Pain. No, it was fear. Janie Ruth looked away from Richard when she said, "She ... Lillie was working there on that Easter Sunday."

"Wow! This is a small world."

"She told me about that day the first time I met her. Lillie was here at Greener Pastures when I got here. She was different. It's been painful watching her and Rose disappear slowly into a rabbit hole."

Lillie asked, "Janie Ruth, who is in a rabbit hole?"

Shocked that Lillie called her by name, Janie Ruth laughed, "Lillie, Lillie? You know who I am?"

Responding as though she had just walked in on the conversation, "Of course, I know who you are Janie Ruth. Do you know who you are?"

They both laughed. Happiness washed over Janie Ruth. Her old friend had resurfaced out of the darkness. Lillie's face was bright. Her eyes were alive, not dark lifeless circles staring out of nothingness. Janie Ruth wondered, *Why now? What happened to make her recognize me now?* Janie Ruth could not contain her happiness. She grabbed Lillie's hand. Looking at Lillie, but speaking to Richard, "She hasn't known who I am or called me by name in a long time."

Confused by Janie Ruth's excitement, Lillie pulled her hand away.

"Lillie, this is Richard. We were just talking about Club Harlem."

Even though he didn't understand the change in Lillie, Richard was excited. *If Lillie has lucid moments, maybe Rose does too,* he thought. Bringing himself back to the moment, he saw the life and beauty that must've been her before the disease invaded her body and mind. She looked nothing like the zombie he saw moments before muttering cigars, cigarettes, Tiparillos. He extended his hand. "It's nice to meet you, Lillie. Janie Ruth tells me you used to be a cigarette girl at Club Harlem."

Giggling and blushing, Lillie looked at Richard. She tilted her head to the side, "Yes, I was. The prettiest one there, too, if I must say so myself. Oh, I had some legs on me. They had cigarette machines there, but the men preferred to buy their cigarettes from the cigarette girls, especially me." Lillie eased herself down into the chair beside Janie Ruth.

Richard was shocked. He looked from Janie Ruth to Lillie. He observed Lillie's drastic transformation with incredulity. He shook his head, smiled, and said, with a hint of nostalgia, "I used to go to Club Harlem."

"Really? Did you smoke? Maybe you bought some smokes from me."

Before Richard could respond, Janie Ruth abruptly interjected, "Lillie, I thought it was a club for Black people."

Throwing her head back, Lillie laughed, "Girl, a lot of white folks came there. When they came to Kentucky and the Curb, they were slumming. They came because they knew they would see a show and hear some music they didn't hear in their white establishments. Pop said Black folk lived in Harlem. White folk came, but it was ours. We, Black folks, didn't have any place that was our own back then; but we had Kentucky and the Curb."

Janie Ruth leaned forward in her seat. Even though she had heard the story before, she asked, "Who was Pop?"

"He was the owner of Club Harlem. Those were the days. I loved working there." Running her hand up and down her right leg, "I had some pretty legs, and the men liked me. I met a lot of performers too. I remember meeting Sam Cooke; he was the nicest man. The music was the best. That club was huge!" Laughing, "They could get about nine hundred people in that place. They could get at least one hundred at that front bar. The club had two bandstands, and the place was always packed, but the summer months were the best and the most exciting because people were there on vacation. The air vibrated with excitement. In the summer, the music would begin on Saturdays at ten o'clock at night and wouldn't stop until six o'clock Monday morning."

Closing his eyes, Richard could almost smell the salty ocean breeze blowing. His favorite times to walk the boardwalk were late night and early morning. They had been times of reflection for him – times to be himself. He chuckled, "I loved coming around two o'clock on Saturday mornings."

Lillie was highly alert as if she had consumed several shots of expresso. She spoke with a sense of urgency, as though she had been allotted a specific time frame to convey her story. "You know there were four shows on Saturday and Sunday nights. There was a ten o'clock show, a midnight show, a two-thirty morning show, and a six o'clock breakfast show. I loved every moment of it. I ... I loved every moment of it."

Richard interjected, "I was telling Janie Ruth I was there the night Fat Ty Palmer was murdered."

"So was I. The place was packed – seven, eight, nine hundred people. Fat Ty sat near the stage, surrounded by a group of pretty girls. I remember walking through his harem of women. This huge bodyguard stepped in front of me. Did I tell you this huge bodyguard stepped in front of me? I looked up at him and smiled. Did I tell you I had some pretty legs? Now what could little me do to Fat Ty?" She smiled and winked at Richard. "I wasn't about to let this big goon stop me from making a sale. So, I slightly turned my body to lean a bit past this goon and catch Fat Ty's attention. When I saw Fat Ty looking. I slowly wet my lips." Before continuing, she looked at Richard and licked her lips. "Then I parted my legs so Fat Ty could see one of my long, beautiful legs. Then I slowly did a little rotation movement of my leg, and I said as sexy as I knew how, cigars, cigarettes, Tiparillos ... cigars, cigarettes, Tiparillos. Fat Ty told his bodyguard to step aside. He looked at me and winked. Wetting my lips again, I smiled. He bought two White Owl Cigars and gave me a fifty-dollar tip."

Richard interjected, "Billy Paul was performing when it happened."

"He sure was. I went to take a bathroom break when Billy Paul was coming out on stage. After using the restroom, I remember standing in the bathroom, looking in the mirror, and swaying to the rhythm of "Magic Carpet Ride." I remember saying to myself it would be nice if there were such a thing as a magic carpet. Just as the song ended, I heard what sounded like a gunshot. Then I heard people screaming and glass breaking. I froze. I could hear my blood pounding in my ears. My legs felt like a wet dishrag. I don't know how my legs managed to move

A Mother's White Lie

me to the door, but they did. I cracked the door and peeped out. I saw people running in every direction. Then I heard two gunshots."

Reliving the story as Lillie told it, Richard said, "Yes! People were pushing, screaming, and knocking over tables and chairs. Plates and glasses shattered on the floor. I was amongst the crowd running. We were suddenly a wall of people pushing, shoving, and trying to get to safety. I almost stepped on a woman who had fallen. I will never forget the fear I saw in her eyes. I managed, without getting trampled, to reach down and yank her from the floor. I held on to her until we reached the door."

Although Janie Ruth had heard this story several times from Lillie, Janie Ruth was anxious to listen to what Richard had to say. "Richard, did you see when he was shot?"

Looking from Lillie to Janie Ruth, Richard said, "No. I only heard the first shot."

Lillie continued talking, "I stayed in the bathroom. I figured it was safe to come out when the gunshots stopped. I peeked out the door and slowly eased out; the police were everywhere. A policeman saw me and asked if I was hurt. I looked at him shaking my head no. My body was shaking like a lightning bolt struck it. I looked around the club. I saw Fat Ty lying in a pool of blood. Tables were turned over. Bottles and glasses were broken. Shoes, pocketbooks, and even jewelry were on the floor. I heard people moaning. One woman looked at me and said, 'I've been shot'. I couldn't help her. I just stood there shaking. I stood there shaking. What was I saying?"

Janie Ruth knew what was coming; she said, "You said there was a lady on the floor, and you stood there shaking."

Lillie said, "Yes, I stood there shaking. The policeman who stopped me stooped down beside her. He told her she would be alright. There were probably nine hundred people at Club Harlem that night, but the police could find no one who would admit to seeing anything. That included me."

Richard added, "The police interviewed me. Five people died that night, and twenty people were injured. No one was ever charged."

Lillie's speech slowed, "You don't know what you can see. You don't ... you don't. Why don't you come with me on a magic carpet ride? Fantasies will set you free."

Janie knew she was gone, but she hoped it would bring her back if she called her name. "Lillie?"

The empty eyes were back. Lillie used her walker to pull herself up from the chair. She looked at Richard and said, "Why are you trying to steal my cigarettes? Cigars, cigarettes, Tiparillos."

Richard sat staring in bewilderment as Lillie walked out of the community room.

Janie Ruth said, "She has gone back into the rabbit hole."

Frowning, Richard asked, "The rabbit hole?"

"Yes. She had a moment of clarity. Now she has retreated into darkness. The rabbit hole."

CHAPTER SIX

Rose

March 1930. The hopeless looked for hope when there was little to none to be found. Being a colored female got Rose work during a time when most colored men were enfolded in the numbness of the unemployed. The Great Depression wasn't good for anyone, but it was especially hard for colored men. They were fired from jobs they had held for years so white men could have work. Rose's mother was a stay-at-home mom before The Great Depression. After Rose's father, Fred, lost his job on the railroad, Rose's mother, Annie, worked as a housekeeper for a white family. Rose was ready and determined to leave her parents' home – an old, dilapidated cannery that sat by the railroad tracks in Rustburg, Virginia. Sharing a room with five sisters, sleeping on a bed tick filled with wheat straw, planting and harvesting corn, beans, potatoes, collards, carrots, and slaughtering hogs in October and November were things Rose wanted to leave behind. "There's no cause to worry about me. The world may be in a panic, but I'm in control of my life." These were the words spewed out of Rose's mouth, to her parents in March 1930, when she decided that she was dropping out of school.

Rose left Rustburg for Lynchburg, Virginia, to seek employment. She stayed with her mother's sister, Rachael, who ran a bootlegging house.

Her aunt resided in a duplex which sat atop a hill, just behind a dilapidated wooden hotel. Rose was fond of her aunt's neighborhood for its vibrancy. Situated on Polk Street, a district inhabited by people of color, it intersected with a red-light district known for its diverse working women. Before the Civil War, these women lived and worked in Buzzards Roost, now Commerce Street, formerly Lynch Street. Following a series of murders and infamous incidents, the police ousted them from their riverfront abodes, prompting a relocation to Fourth, Monroe, and Taylor Streets.

The street was never empty. A Baptist church was nestled close to her aunt's backyard. On summer Sundays when Rose didn't attend the service, she would sit on the back steps, letting the gospel hymns drift to her on the warm breeze. On the occasions she did go, she often encountered her Aunt Rachael's customers. They would depart from the church, hearts brimming with the Holy Spirit, and then visit her aunt to indulge in spirits of a different kind.

In need of employment, Rose was referred by her Aunt Rachael to Susan Weinstein, whose office was behind Robert E. Lee Junior High School on Park Avenue. Susan informed Rose that, due to her lack of prior job experience, she would need to compensate her five dollars weekly for three months for the employment assistance. Susan advised Rose to work diligently to build her professional references.

Susan placed her in the residence of Doctor Charles and Margaret Blair. Charles was rarely home, and Margaret hosted tea parties and attended meetings.

Rose made ten dollars a week. She didn't always receive her full pay in cash. Sometimes she was paid with leftover food from the Blair family or clothes they no longer wanted. After Rose gave Susan five dollars, there were some weeks when Rose only had leftover food and used clothes to show for a week of hard work. She hated it when Margaret did that. She wanted to quit but remembered what Susan said about establishing references.

Rose walked five miles on her first day to get to her job. After looking up and down the street and determining she was in the right place and on the right side of the street, she turned and continued walking up Rivermont Avenue. When she got to the area, she looked around at all the beautiful houses. She pulled a piece of paper from her pocket and looked at the address on it. The address she was looking for was five houses from where she had stopped. Filled with trepidation and excitement, she walked down five houses to reach her destination. Again, checking the address, she stood on the sidewalk staring up at a Queen-Anne-style house. The lawn was vibrant green, and every blade of grass was evenly cut. Azaleas were in bloom around the porch, which wrapped around the house. The turrets that projected vertically from the corner of the house reminded Rose of castles she had seen in fairy tale books.

Margaret was about to go into the house when she noticed Rose staring in her direction. She called her son, "Charlie, go out there and see why that colored gal is staring at our house."

Tall and slender, Charlie took long strides toward Rose as he asked her, "Are you looking for someone?"

Looking at the man approaching her, Rose's mind told her to run, but her legs refused to move. Overcome with fear, she stood like a statute. Fear gagged her, so she said nothing. Charlie stopped right in front of her. He towered over her. She could feel his eyes burning through the top of her head. Feeling uncomfortable, she wanted to look up, but he was white, and she didn't want to disrespect him by making eye contact. Her body was tense. Charlie reached out and touched her shoulder. It was a soft touch. She felt her tension ease a bit. He smiled and repeated his question, "Are you looking for someone?"

She could hear his smile in his voice, and it eased her fear even more. With her head still bowed, Rose handed him the piece of paper with the house address and Susan Weinstein's name written on it. Charlie looked at the paper and said, "You're in the right place. What's your name?"

"Rose." Her voice was barely audible.

"Rose, do you have a last name?"

She bowed her head, smiling, "Yes, sir, Franklin. Rose Franklin."

"My name is Charlie Blair. Follow me, and I'll take you to my mother. She's the person you're looking for."

Rose walked behind him, almost stepping on his heels. He led her up the front steps to the porch.

Upset with her son for bringing a colored girl to her front step, Margaret asked, "What are you doing, Charlie?"

Charlie responded, "Susan sent her."

Margaret looked her up and down and said, "I wasn't expecting her until tomorrow. Take her around back."

"Mother don't be ridiculous. She's right here. We're right here. Let her come in the front door."

"Okay but get her in here before someone sees her entering my front door."

Charlie held the door. Rose stood waiting for Charlie to go in before her. He leaned down and peered into her face. He smiled and waved, gesturing for her to enter the house before him. Rose hesitantly walked through the front door and into the formal entrance hall, her head still bowed. She was amazed at the size; the entrance hall was larger than her aunt's house.

Margaret turned to her, "What is your name, gal?"

"Rose Franklin, ma'am."

"Hold your head up, gal, so I can see your face." Margaret was a stout woman with a large nose and curly shoulder-length brown hair with grey highlights. With an air of arrogant dignity, Margaret looked at Rose and said, "You're to use the back door, not the front door." Margaret looked at her son, who excused himself and went up one side of the grand double staircase to the second floor. A massive crystal chandelier hung between the staircases. She turned to Rose, asking, "Do you understand?"

"Yes, ma'am." Rose's stomach was in knots. Listening to Margaret, Rose wondered, *how will I be able to work for this woman? She is a mean snob! It seems like she is looking right through me like I'm invisible.*

"Gal! Are you listening to me?"

"Yes, ma'am." Rose hoped Mrs. Blair could not see how badly her body trembled.

"Follow me to the kitchen."

"Yes, ma'am."

Margaret led Rose through the vestibule to the kitchen in the back of the house. Margaret introduced Rose to the cook, Sadie, a sturdy-built older woman with a broad face and high cheekbones. Sadie didn't turn to look at Rose. She never stopped stirring the grits she was cooking but nodded her head to acknowledge Rose. Margaret informed Rose she would be responsible for cleaning the house and doing the laundry. "Sadie will answer any questions you may have."

Rose looked at Sadie, hoping she would turn around and give her a look or gesture that would put her at ease. Sadie never looked at her. Rose nervously wiped her hands down the side of her skirt and responded with another, "Yes, ma'am."

CHAPTER SEVEN

Rose

April 1930. Rose saw motion but no real movement. Margaret was busy with meetings. Her husband, Charles, ate breakfast and grunted goodbye as he left for his office in the mornings. Charlie was in and out of the house throughout the day. Rose was not sure of what he did. Everyone was always busy doing something, but life in the Blair house seemed stagnant. No warmth or love was shared by the people who lived in it.

Rose wondered why Margaret had hired her. Margaret only seemed happy when she was attacking her. One morning, just as Rose had completed folding the laundry, Margaret entered the room smiling.

"Rose, I had a little accident in the bathroom. Would you be a dear and clean it up?"

"Yes, ma'am."

When Rose approached the bathroom door, a stench greeted her nostrils, causing her to gag. When she opened the door, she could not believe what she saw – feces was smeared all over the toilet seat and floor. Quickly closing the door, tears welled up in her eyes, she couldn't understand how a grown, sophisticated woman could be so mean and nasty. Standing with her back pressed against the door, she convinced herself matters could be worse.

Her Aunt Rachael had cautioned her about the potential risks of working as a domestic. Before starting her bootleg business, Rachael did domestic work. Her madam's husband took indecent liberties with her. The wife knew what her husband was doing but she remained silent until Rachael's pregnancy became apparent. Then one day when Rachael was carrying a laundry basket downstairs, the wife walked up behind her and shoved her. Rachael lost the baby, and she almost died. Rachael said she never reported what had happened to authorities because a Colored person's word against a white person was never believed.

Rose covered her nose and mouth with the scarf she had tied around her head, opened the bathroom door, and cleaned the toilet seat and the floor with bleach. When she returned to put away the folded laundry, she found the clothes scattered about the table. Margaret was standing by the table with a sheepish grin.

"I was looking for something. Rose, you need to be a dear and fold these again."

Rose smiled and said, "Yes, ma'am."

She was not being molested and needed the job, so she went about her duties with her head bowed and mouth closed. She accepted she was Margaret's target.

There were three floors of rooms to clean, windows to wash, clothes to launder and hang out to dry. Then there was laundry to iron, fold, and put away. By mid-April, Rose had established a schedule and routine to complete her responsibilities and get off by six o'clock.

One morning towards the end of April, Rose arrived at the Blair house to learn that Sadie wasn't there. Sadie's mother had died of a heart attack during the night. Margaret informed Rose that she would be responsible for preparing the meals and cleaning during Sadie's absence without additional pay. She told Rose she should consider it as part of her reference building. Rose had no choice but to smile and say, "Yes, ma'am." Cooking wasn't something Rose often did, but she felt she could handle it; she did it along with her other duties. During the day, Rose hadn't had a moment to think about the time. She put the last dish away and realized it was nine o'clock. While she stood looking out the kitchen window and dreading the walk home in the dark, Charlie came into the kitchen.

"Rose…." She jumped. Charlie laughed, "I didn't mean to scare you. I thought you could use a ride home."

"No sir, I don't need a ride."

Charlie smiled, "Don't be ridiculous. It's late, and it's dark."

"Yes, sir, but I'll be alright. Mrs. Blair…."

"Tonight is Mother's bridge night. My father is making some house calls. So, get your things together. I'll take you home."

She felt she shouldn't argue with a white man. So, she said, "Yes, sir. Thank you, Mr. Charlie."

Rose gathered her belongings and started to walk towards the back door. Charlie quickly stepped in front of her to open it. Rose stood waiting for Charlie to go out first, but he reached for her arm to assist her over the door sill. As she stepped outside, the thick warm night air smelling of honeysuckle invaded her nostrils. When she got to the car, Charlie was holding the front door open on the passenger's side of his black Duesenberg. Rose glanced up at him. She wasn't sure what to think about how Charlie treated her. He was treating her like she was a white girl. She slid into the car. He closed the door, ran around, and got into the driver's seat. She started to give him directions.

"I know where you live. I know the area well."

She wondered why this white man was so familiar with a colored neighborhood. She thought maybe *he was a patron of the red-light district.* She smiled and sat quietly, holding her purse and a brown paper bag containing remnants of her lunch. When he pulled up in front of her aunt's house, she started to open the car door.

"Wait, I'll get the door for you."

Annoyed at the thought she needed help opening a car door, she said, "I am not helpless. I can open it."

"I know you aren't helpless and can open a car door, but you shouldn't have to." Charlie chuckled. This was refreshing to him. All the other females, who had been in his car, expected him to jump out of the car and open the door.

Frowning, she asked, "Why shouldn't I?"

He smiled and responded, "Because you are a lady."

He thinks I'm a lady, she thought. Not knowing what to say, she didn't move. She just stared at her lap. She could feel him looking at her. Her mind immediately returned to her Aunt Rachael's experience as a domestic. *Is this the way it starts? Will he force himself on me?* A sudden feeling of claustrophobia washed over her like a cocoon.

"Rose, I think you're so pretty."

Her eyes widened. She was stunned. A white man was telling her she was pretty. Rose slowly lifted her head to look at him. She was seeing him for the first time. He was handsome, a better-looking version of his father. He got out of the car and opened the door for her. She didn't know what to think about the way Charlie was acting. She stepped out of the vehicle.

Nervously she said, "Thank you, Mr. Charlie."

"You are welcome. Have a good evening."

Midway up the steps to her aunt's front door, Rose realized she hadn't heard Charlie's car drive away. When she turned to look behind her, Charlie was watching her from his car. Rose turned and ran up the remaining seven steps and opened the front door. Before stepping inside, she again looked behind her. Charlie waved to her. She walked into the house and closed the door. When she cracked the door to peep out, Charlie was gone. Although it was unsettling, she liked the attention Charlie had shown her. It made her feel special.

Rose did double duty for a week. That meant Charlie took her home every evening for five days. During those five days, she learned Charlie's parents were not home most evenings. He learned she was very close to her parents. She learned Charlie's name was Charles. He learned she was the third child of ten children. She learned he wasn't very close to his father. He learned she loved to read. She learned he worked in real estate and owned several houses in her aunt's neighborhood. He learned she loved playing the piano and sometimes played in church. She learned he was twenty-five years old, and he learned she was sixteen. He was never once improper with her.

CHAPTER EIGHT

Rose

May 1930. Sadie's return to work was met with mixed feelings from Rose. She was glad to give up the extra duties, but it also meant giving up rides home from Charlie. But Charlie found ways to be in the same space with Rose as often as he could. They exchanged looks and secret touches in passing causing them both to shiver with excitement. The weekends were theirs. Closing out the world, they stole time together. Neither age nor race stopped the development of a friendship that rapidly turned into an intimate relationship.

Even though they tried to hide their relationship, it was obvious to Sadie that something was going on. It was on a Friday; Sadie was watching out the kitchen window at Rose taking clothes from the clothesline when Charlie came up behind Rose and tickled her on her sides. They laughed, and Charlie said something to Rose before he entered the house. Sadie quickly moved from the window. She grabbed the broom and started sweeping the kitchen floor. Charlie walked through the kitchen whistling.

"Hi, Sadie."

"Hello, Mr. Charlie." She stood watching after him shaking her head.

Even though Rose and Sadie had not become friends, Sadie's maternal instinct wanted to protect her. Rose came in singing with a laundry basket of clothes under one arm. Sadie stepped in her path. "Child, I don't know what happened while I was gone, but whatever it was, you need to put an end to it now. Do you hear me, child?"

Rose hesitated before saying, "I don't know what you're talking about, Sadie."

Sadie replied emphatically, "I'm telling you child; you're walking down a dangerous road."

"I don't know what you mean by that. I need to fold and put the laundry away."

"You can't think he means you good. Don't say I didn't try to warn you."

Rose smiled at Sadie. As she left the kitchen, she turned and said, "Thank you."

Sadie looked over her shoulder at Rose and shook her head.

When six o'clock rolled around, Rose and Sadie gathered their things to get off for the weekend. Charlie came into the kitchen.

"My mother had to attend a meeting this evening. She asked me to give you your pay." He gave each of them an envelope with their name on it. They both thanked him and left together.

When Rose got home to her Aunt Rachael's, several men were sitting around a table in the living room area laughing. At the table, there was a chair draped in black. Her Aunt Rachael explained one of her regular patrons died earlier in the week. His friends had just completed a ceremony retiring his drinking glass. She pointed to the glass sitting on a shelf with the glasses of several other patrons who had also passed on to the other side of life. There was a genuine camaraderie among the men who visited her aunt's establishment. Those fortunate enough to have jobs would often buy a round of drinks for unemployed friends. Rose spoke and the men in the room exchanged looks as she turned to go to her room. When she opened her envelope, she found a twenty-dollar bill and a note: *Meet me at our special place on Saturday at three o'clock.* She laid the money and the note on the bed. She stood in front of the mirror looking at her reflection. She heard Sadie's voice saying *I'm telling you child; you're walking down a dangerous road. You can't think he means you good. Don't say I didn't warn you.*

CHAPTER NINE

Rose

Rose woke up Saturday morning smiling. She couldn't wait to see Charlie. She wanted to look special for him; she didn't want her aunt to ask her where she was going. Her priority was getting into the bathroom early before her aunt's Saturday regulars started coming in for drinks and conversation. As she sank into the warm bath water in the galvanized tub, she could feel Charlie's warm embrace. She thought about their first time together. Charlie had an empty rental house just two blocks from her aunt. That was their special place. The first time they met there he brought her a single rose, and she gave him what she hadn't given any man before him. Smiling, she slid further down into the warm water as she relived their first time together.

He had been so gentle. He opened the door for her and he handed her a single rose. He had candles lit all around the room. Rose petals were scattered about the floor. In the middle of the room was a mattress covered with a white sheet and rose petals. He led her to the center of the room and lowered her to a mattress. They talked for hours about their dreams. He kissed her, took her by the hands, and pulled her up. They were both nervous. She shivered.

Putting his arms around her, he asked, "Are you cold?"

"No, I'm just nervous. I've never done this before."

"Me either."

She had been surprised by his comment. So, she asked, "You're a virgin?"

"No. I mean, I've never...."

"Made love to a Colored girl."

"Well, uh...."

"Let's not talk."

They both took a deep breath to relax. He unbuttoned her dress and started to slide it off her shoulders, she closed her eyes. Her dress fell to the floor around her feet. He then slipped the straps of her slip off her shoulders. She placed her hands on his to stop him when he reached for her bra straps. He gently kissed Rose on her forehead and worked his way down to her lips.

"Please, let me see all of you."

She slowly moved her hands from his. He embraced her, unhooked her bra, and slid the straps down her arms. Embracing her again, he ran his hands down her back and into her panties. He slowly knelt as he slid them down to her feet. He kissed her stomach and then her breasts. He circled her dark nipples with his fingers. She shivered with delight. He kissed each breast. Then he stepped back from her. She stood like a statute with her eyes closed.

"You're so beautiful."

She opened her eyes. "You think I'm beautiful?"

"Yes." He reached for her hands and pulled her to him and kissed her. She helped him undress. She had never seen a naked man before, and here was a white man standing before her naked. She remembered thinking to herself his body was whiter than his face. He gently picked her up in his arms and laid her on the mattress. Feeling the heat of his body, she wrapped her legs around him.

Rose shivered. The water was getting cool, so she stepped out of the tub, dried herself, and went to her room. Applying lotion all over her body, she was ready to dress. Charlie liked her in red, so she put on a red printed dress. She put her hair up because she liked it when he took it down. When she exited her room, it was two-forty-five and her aunt's house was already busy with people drinking, laughing, and playing cards. She stopped in the hallway when she heard her Aunt Rachael talking with someone with a deep raspy voice.

Her Aunt Rachael cleared her throat. "I know what you are saying. But you know how young folk are."

"Yeah, I know, but Rachael, she needs to be careful. How long can we wear the mask? We smile saying 'Yes, sir.' They take our jobs. We say, 'Yes, sir.' They sleep with our women. We say, 'Yes, sir.' They own houses in our neighborhood, so they think they own us. And we say, 'Yes sir.' Tell her to stay out of the line of fire."

Rose felt they were talking about her and Charlie, but she wondered what the person meant by staying out of the line of fire. She coughed so they would know she was in the hallway. Most of her aunt's patrons were men trying to shake off the dust of weariness and gloom from trying to make ends meet. When Rose got to the door of the room where the voices were coming from, she saw her aunt and three men playing cards. Rose did not recognize any of them as her aunt's regulars. The men all nodded to her as she passed.

The words 'tell her to stay out of the line of fire' twirled around through her head. She did not like the sound of what she had heard. She tried to shake the feeling of dread that washed over her when she heard the words. With her destination only a few blocks away, she decided she would rid herself of any bad feelings by taking in the beauty of her neighborhood. As she passed Lucille Watson's house, she noticed the colored bottles, mostly blue, stuck in the ground on both sides of her walkway. Rose remembered her grandma, Delia Nowlin, a former slave, talking about how bottle trees kept haints from entering a house. Grandma Delia told them haints that would carouse around at night, were attracted to the glitter of glass, and would enter the bottles and get stuck. Then they would be destroyed by the morning sun. Seeing Lucille's bottles made Rose chuckle out loud because there was no way haints could get into her bottles stuck in the ground.

The Johnson house had marigolds in a flowerbox on the front porch. The beauty in her neighborhood was unlike what she saw in the neighborhood where Charlie lived. The beauty of her neighbors' yards was natural and familiar. Charlie's car was already at their special place when she arrived. Neighbors were sitting on their porches. Three older women were sitting on the porch next door to the house that was their special place. Rose smiled and spoke. The women spoke but exchanged raised eyebrow looks with one another. Stepping on the porch, Rose could smell different aromas of sweetness the Sweet Peas and Snap Dragons were emitting. She felt eyes watching as she took a deep breath and smiled. When she reached for the doorknob, the door opened. The neighbors across the street were watching with an 'oh child' look. The next-door neighbors leaned forward in their chairs, trying to see. Charlie grabbed Rose's hand, waved at the neighbors across the street, pulled Rose inside the house, and closed the door. When the door closed, the neighbors' tongues started wagging faster than a dog's tail welcoming his master home after a long day away. Charlie hugged Rose and kissed her lightly on the lips.

"Close your eyes."

"Why?"

"I have a surprise for you." Charlie put his hands over her eyes. Walking behind her, he led her into the next room. "Don't peek. Keep your eyes closed." He took his hands from her eyes and stepped in front of her. "Open your eyes." When she opened her eyes, she saw Charlie standing before her. He leaned down and gently kissed her on the lips. Then he stepped aside, and she saw a piano. She screamed with joy. She kissed him, ran over to the piano, and began to play. He sat beside her on the piano bench as she played and sang over my head, I hear music in the air.

He enjoyed listening to her play and sing. He especially liked the song she was singing because he heard music when he was with her. When she finished playing, he kissed her again. Then he told her he had another surprise. He went into another room and brought out a picnic basket. He put a blanket on the floor; and he laid out cheese sandwiches, apples, grapes, soda pop, and a bottle of wine. They sat on the blanket and ate sandwiches and drank wine. It was Rose's first time drinking wine, and it made her feel warm and tingly inside. He pulled her to him. He ran his hands under her dress and between her legs. She trembled with excitement. He washed her body with his tongue. She helped him remove his shirt and trousers. He gently entered her igniting a flame that turned into a burning inferno of passion.

She looked up at him and asked, "Is it always going to be like this?"

"Yes, for you ... for us, it will be. I was your first, and I don't want you experiencing anyone but me."

"I don't want anyone else but you." She smiled and snuggled under him. Lying in his arms, she wondered if she should tell him about what she heard earlier. She decided against it. They fell asleep in each other's arms.

CHAPTER TEN

Rose

After a weekend with Charlie, Rose felt she could endure anything his mother did or said. She felt a happiness in her heart she had never felt before. She had an ache in her gut – an ache she got when she was overcome with fear. The last time she felt that fear was when she found a black snake coiled under the steps of her parents' house the day before she told her parents she was moving to Lynchburg.

When Rose arrived at work, the aromas from the kitchen of fried country ham and red-eyed gravy competed with the scents of the magnolias and lilacs in the backyard. That delicious aroma meant Sadie had gotten to work early. It also meant the Blair family was probably having breakfast together. Rose had come in several mornings when the family was silent at the table. They only spoke or even looked at one another when asking for something.

Rose could see Sadie, through the screen door, wiping sweat from her ebony face. Sadie looked over her shoulder when she heard the screen door open.

"Morning, Rose."

"Good morning, Sadie. How're you on this beautiful morning?"

"There's nothing good about this here morning, little girl. Mr. Charlie just went storming out of here. I tried to warn you that you were traveling down a dangerous road, but you didn't listen. Miss Margaret been waiting for you."

Rose froze. Happiness suddenly left her heart to join the fear she felt in her gut. "Should I go back home?"

Before Sadie could say anything, Margaret stormed into the kitchen like a bull ready to charge. Her face was crimson and her demeanor formidable. A prominent vein protruded from the middle of her temple and from both sides of her neck.

Rose stood with her back to the screen door. She saw what she imagined to be a reincarnation of Satan. She wanted to run, but before she could move on her own, Margaret was in her face screaming and pushing her out of the screen door.

Snorting, Margaret screamed, "Get out of my house! Leave!"

Rose's body stiffened against Margaret's efforts to continue pushing her. Rose opened her mouth to speak, but nothing came out. She swallowed and questioningly responded, "Ma'am?"

"Don't ma'am me. You heard me! Leave! Your services are no longer needed!"

"But Ma'am, I don't understand!"

"Oh, you understand! You, nigger bitch! Leave my son alone!"

Rose's fear turned to anger, an anger that brought her out of submission mode. She and Margaret were standing face to face. Rose slowly lifted her head. She looked Margaret in her eyes, and through clenched teeth and slightly opened lips, she stated slowly and deliberately, "Ma'am, I'm not a nigger or a bitch."

Rose's tone prompted Margaret to step back. Rose could see Sadie standing behind Margaret. Rose looked from Margaret to Sadie. Sadie lowered her head and slowly turned back to the stove. Tears fell from her eyes, intermingling with her sweat.

Rose backed away from Margaret and left.

CHAPTER ELEVEN

Rose

July 1930. They had flirted with the devil, so, they were bound to be burned or singed. Mid-July, Rose realized she was pregnant. She was scared. What was she going to do? Her first thought was to move back home with her parents. When she shared the news of her pregnancy with her mother and father, her father told her she wasn't welcome back home.

Rose's father was a scrawny man with a salt and pepper beard. His skin was leathery from years of working in the sun on the railroad. "I told ja and yo sisters if ya go and got ya'self-pregnant, ya can't stay here! I'se got enouf mouths to feed and here ya gone and got ya'self-pregnant by a cracker!" Being pregnant was one thing but being pregnant by a white man was something he couldn't forgive. He poured himself a glass of dandelion wine and took a big gulp before he spoke again. "How could ja do dis to us? How could ja do it to ya'self? As soon as dat cracker gits mad with ja he'll be calling ya all kinds of niggas. Jus' like his Mammy! Did ja fo'git I lost my job 'cause some cracker needed a job? Did ja fo'git dat we livin' here in dis cannery because Rachael and ya Granny Sarah let some cracker talk dem into sellin' our house and all de family property from under us?" Rose's father ranted on not giving her a chance to respond. "I'se sure as I'se knows my name, yo' Ant Rachael ain't gonna continue letting you stay der wif hur. Annie, talk to de girl 'cuz I don't wanna have a damn thang to do wif hur!"

Before his wife could say anything, he stormed out of the room, slamming the door, leaving Rose with her mother.

Rose's mother looked at her and said, "Honey, your dad is right. You done made your bed. Now you gonna have to lay in it. Have you told the baby's father? What you gonna do?"

"Charlie ... Charlie is the father. No, I haven't told him. I'm not sure of what I'm going to do. I guess the first thing is to tell Charlie. Mama, I believe he loves me. He continued seeing me even though he knew his mother was against it. Mama, I know I love him."

Rose's mother hugged her. "Well, baby, I guess you'll soon find out if he loves you."

Hurting her parents was the last thing Rose wanted to do. Awkward silence invaded the room and became a temporary wall between Rose and her mother. *Color shouldn't have anything to do with the person I love. Charlie didn't take Daddy's job. Charlie didn't talk Aunt Rachael and Granny into selling the family property. It's not Charlie's fault.*

Shattering the silence, Rose's mother took her daughter's hands in her own, "Rose, you know your daddy and I love you."

"I know."

"We just want better for you. I didn't finish school, and your daddy never learned to read."

Rose could not look at her mother. She knew she loved Charlie, but she was feeling some shame; not because Charlie was white but because she had disappointed her parents.

"Rose, I also have some news for you."

"What is it?"

Her mother dropped Rose's hand and put her hands on her own stomach, and said, "I guess you should know you're going to have another brother or sister."

"Oh, Mama."

"I know, number eleven. It sounds like we're due around the same time. I'll be in Lynchburg to see you in the next two weeks. We'll talk more then."

Rose kissed her mother goodbye. She walked down the dirt road to her Uncle Floyd's house. He was her ride back to Lynchburg. As she walked kicking rocks, she remembered her words to her parents the day she left home. *There is no cause to worry about me. The world may be in a panic, but I'm in control of my life.* Now she was in a panic. Her father had turned his back on her, and her mother was pregnant. She did not utter one word on the ride back.

Climbing the fifteen concrete steps to the porch, at her Aunt Rachael's house, felt like climbing Mount Everest. *Aunt Rachael has to help me,* she thought. Her aunt's boisterous laughter, followed by "Ouch, that was my ear" greeted her when she entered the front door. Rose walked down the hall to the kitchen. There, she found her aunt sitting in a chair by the wood stove. Miss Edna, a tall, slender, masculine-looking woman with a cigarette, more ash than cigarette, hanging from her lips, was standing behind her aunt. Rachael had her head down, with her right hand folding and holding her right ear down. Miss Edna had a glob of hair grease on the back of her left hand and a hot straightening comb in her right hand. She blew vigorously as the hair grease in Rachael's hair sizzled, meeting the hot comb.

Rose spoke, "Good evening."

Both women returned her greeting. Rose had hoped to find her aunt alone.

Looking up at Rose, "She is burning out the little hair I have left." Rachael exclaimed.

"You need to be still if you don't want me to burn your ear again," Miss Edna retorted.

Rose chuckled. She stood for a moment, waiting for the ash from Miss Edna's cigarette to fall; it didn't. When she turned to go to her room, her father's words, *I'se sure as I knows my name, yo' Ant Rachael ain't gonna continue letting you stay der wif her,* were ringing in her ears. *Aunt Rachael can't put me out,* she thought. *But what if she does? What am I going to do?*

* * *

Three weeks passed before she mustered up the courage to tell Charlie she was pregnant. She got to their special place before Charlie. She walked around trying to decide how she was going to tell him. As she looked around, she thought, *this special place doesn't feel so special right now.* She heard Charlie's key in the door. When Charlie came in, she was sitting on the piano bench. He put his hands on her shoulders. When he leaned down to kiss her, she pulled away.

Confused by her response to his touch, he stood up and asked, "What's wrong, honey?"

She turned away from him and started to cry.

"Look at me, Rose." She slowly lifted her head. He could see the tears rolling down her face. "Please tell me why you're crying."

She opened her mouth to speak, but nothing came out. He reached for her, and she pulled away again, and in between the sobs, she uttered the dreaded words, "I'm pregnant."

He turned away from her and walked over to the window. Fingering with the curtains, he took a deep breath. He knew his parents, especially his mother, would be angry. He was scared, but he loved Rose.

She wanted to see his face, but he stood with his back to her. Silence engulfed the room and forced itself into her being, painfully squeezing her like the arms of a giant octopus. Her fear was like bile rising in her throat, choking her. She grabbed her chest. She was having a hard time breathing. *Why did he walk away from me? Why won't he look at me?* She feared he was going to leave her. She hadn't considered what she would do if Charlie told her he didn't want her or the baby.

He finally spoke and his voice was void of emotion. "Are you sure?"

"I haven't seen a doctor, nor have I been pregnant before, but I'm pretty sure. I've missed my period for two months." He turned from the window. He was looking at her, but she could not tell what he was thinking from his face. Holding her chest, she started crying uncontrollably. "I'm so sorry."

"Don't cry." He walked over to her and gently pulled her off the piano bench into his arms. "Rose, I love you."

Catching her breath, she said, "I love you too, Charlie, but love is not enough. What are we going to do?"

He released his embrace and stepped back from her. "You're going to move in here. I will furnish this place."

Her fear was suddenly compounded with anger. With a clenched fist, Rose stood staring at Charlie. With much indignation, she asked, "I'll move in here?"

Shocked by the sudden change in her tone, "I didn't mean it like that. I'll be here with you. Rose, I want to marry you."

Charlie and Rose had never argued. She did not like the way she was feeling but Charlie's response was not pragmatic.

Her voice raised an octave, "Look at us, Charlie! Are you crazy? I'm colored, and you're white! Who's gonna marry us?"

They both knew their relationship was against the law. Virginia had Racial Integrity Laws which prohibited relationships and marriage between colored and white people.

Space continued to separate them. "I know, but that won't stop us from being together."

"Charlie, your parents aren't happy with you now. Like thieves, we steal moments together." Sarcasm wrapped tightly in fear and anger, she chuckled and inquired, "You're going to be here with me? What will your mother say? You know how she feels about me."

He knew what Rose was saying was true. His mother would never accept her or any children he had with Rose. But he needed to assure Rose that everything was going to be alright. "I'm my own man. It's not going to be easy, but we are going to be together."

Looking at him shaking her head, "You keep saying that."

Frowning, he asked, "Saying what?"

"We're going to be together. Are you trying to convince yourself or me?"

Charlie didn't respond to her question. He moved closer to her, took out his wallet, and gave her some money. "I want you to see a doctor as soon as possible. I want you and our baby to be healthy." He pulled her into his arms and held her so tight he could feel her heart beating and her body trembling against his. "Are you scared?"

She allowed herself to be comforted by his embrace. "Yes, aren't you? Charlie, what are we going to do?"

"Yes, I'm scared, but we'll be alright. Come with me." He kissed her lightly on her lips. They fell asleep in each other's embrace on their special mattress in their special place.

* * *

Rose and Charlie decided in two weeks they would be living together in their special place. Rose never imagined she would be in this situation with any man, nonetheless a white man. No longer having to worry about rejection, she could now let her Aunt Rachael know she was pregnant, and she would be moving out of her house. She found her aunt in the kitchen washing shot glasses.

"Aunt Rachael, I need to talk to you."

"Good morning, child. What's on your mind?"

"Aunt Rachael, I'm moving out."

Rachael looked at her and laughed. "Where are you going?"

Rose smiled, "I'm not going far. Just up the street."

"Child, you know you have tongues wagging all over this neighborhood."

Mumbling to herself, "I don't care what people are saying. People are going to always find something or somebody to talk about." Not wanting to hear what else she thought her aunt might say to her, Rose walked out of the kitchen.

Her aunt called after her. "Rose, where are you going?"

"To my room. I need to finish packing."

Rachael wiped her hands on her apron and followed Rose. She stood in the door of Rose's room. "Your mother told me when she came by the other day you were thinking about moving."

Taking her clothes out of the dresser drawers and placing them in a box, Rose smiled, "Aunt Rachael, I'm pregnant."

Rachael laughed, "Oh, lord have mercy, child, I know!"

Placing lotion and perfume from the dresser carefully underneath her clothing, "Mama told you that too, huh?

"Yes, but I already suspected. Rose, she's worried about you. You know tongues are going to wag, don't you?"

Rubbing her stomach, Rose replied, "I don't care what people say!"

"Rose, you need to care. No one is happy about the two of you being together." Rachael and Rose stood looking at one another in silence. "Rose, you're just a kid!"

"I guess I'm a woman now!" Surveying the room to make sure she had not forgotten anything, "Daddy has turned his back on me. I don't know what I would do if I didn't have Mama to talk to. I hope you will not turn your back on me too. You know I'm going to need a midwife."

Rachael had delivered Rose and several of her siblings. "And you know I'll be there for you. And if you ever need someplace to go, my door is always open."

Rose stopped packing and looked at Rachael. "Do you think he will leave me?"

"I didn't say that. I just want you to know you always have someplace you can call home."

Rachael helped her pack the rest of her things. Rose took them to her special place with Charlie. The neighbors whispered about Rose and Charlie, but they seemed to accept him in the Tinbridge

Hill neighborhood with open arms. After all, some of them were living in houses Charlie owned.

CHAPTER TWELVE

Rose

Envy was not adorned in a cloak of jealousy; instead, envy was bejeweled in a garment of resentment and want. Charlie made sure Rose had everything she needed and most of what she wanted. He furnished the house with all the latest appliances. The neighbors sat on their porches and watched furniture, rugs, and kitchen appliances being delivered. Rose and Charlie's house had the only telephone on the street. The unctuous neighbors used every excuse they could to see the inside of Rose and Charlie's home. They checked on her because she was pregnant; they borrowed sugar; they shared their baked goods; they asked to use the telephone; and they talked about her when they left. The neighbors were envious of what she had but were not jealous of who they thought she was. They saw her as a kept woman - a white man's bed warmer – a white man's servant.

Jennifer Lipford Petticolas

* * *

Early on February 3, 1931, back pain prevented Rose from sleeping. She felt if she could walk, it would help alleviate her pain. At three forty-five that morning, she quietly slipped out of bed so as not to disturb Charlie. Her mouth was dry. Holding on to the wall for support, she descended the stairs and slowly went to the kitchen. Just as she opened the Frigidaire door, pain erupted in the lower part of her stomach. She opened her mouth to scream, but there was no sound. Rose felt like someone had knocked the breath out of her. She stood bent over, holding on to the open Frigidaire door. She was afraid to breathe. As the pain subsided, she slowly stood up and went to the living room. Just as she was easing herself onto the sofa, she felt a warm gush of fluid running down her legs. Rose called out for Charlie. He stumbled out of bed and almost fell down the stairs. He found her on her hands and knees when he got to the living room. He looked down and realized he was standing in a puddle of water.

"What happened? Did you spill something?" Rose did not respond, but she let out a blood-curdling scream as he reached down to help her off the floor. Startled, he stepped back. She yelled for him to leave her alone when he attempted to touch her again. He glanced at her face and noticed it was wet with sweat and tears. He was unsure of what he should do. He decided to make a telephone call. While speaking into the receiver, he heard Rose scream.

"Get my Aunt Rachael! Get my Aunt Rachael!"

Trying to be obedient in getting her what she needed, he said to the person on the other end of the receiver. "Please hurry." He hung up the phone and put on his shoes. The cold, wet winter air brushed his face when he opened the door.

Just as he was leaving, she cried, "I'm scared! I'm scared! Don't leave me!"

He stopped, turned back, and took her hand in his. He was battling to hide his anxiety. This was uncharted territory for him. He had never seen a woman in labor. He kissed her and assured her he would be right back. When he stepped outside, freezing droplets of rain were falling like diamonds from the dark early morning sky. He could see his breath as he ran the two blocks to Rachael's house. The street was empty. He slipped and fell as he tried to run up the fifteen concrete steps leading to the house. He felt his right elbow and both knees stinging. He banged on the door.

Rachael yelled, "I'm not open. Come back later."

"Miss Rachael, it's me! Charlie! Rose is having the baby. She needs you!"

Rachael opened the door. Charlie was standing there wet from head to toe.

"Where's your coat? Who's with her?"

"I didn't have time to get it. No one is with her."

"Get back there. I'll be right behind you."

Charlie ran down the steps and up the street. Rachael got her black bag, her coat, and a rain cap. She walked quickly up the street. When Rachael arrived at the house, a tall white man with a doctor's bag was getting out of a car. Three heads were peering out of the next-door neighbor's front window, and the neighbor from across the street was standing on her porch in a robe and slippers. She yelled, "Is everything alright over there?"

Rachael dismissed her with a wave of her hand. The man with the doctor's bag acknowledged Rachael with a nod but ignored the neighbors. He opened the gate and stepped aside to let Rachael enter. He followed Rachael to the porch. As Rachael reached for the doorknob, they heard Rose screaming, "Mom! Mom! It hurts! Make it stop!"

Rachael called out for Charlie. He emerged from the bedroom and ran down the stairs. He was as white as a sheet. Charlie saw Rachael and his father standing in the living room. He shook his father's hand, quickly introduced him to Rachael, and told them when he returned from Rachael's house, he found Rose in the bedroom biting into the pillow with each contraction. Charlie led them upstairs. When he opened the bedroom door, Rose was sitting in the bed hugging a pillow. Her eyes widened when she saw Charlie's father. The sight of Charles Blair magnified her fear. She dropped the pillow and slid down in the bed.

Realizing what she must be feeling, Charlie tried to assure her everything was alright. "Rose, it's alright. I called him. He is here to help."

Just as the words rolled through Charlie's lips, Rose was overcome by a painful contraction that caused her to writhe in discomfort on the bed. At that moment, she didn't care who was there. Her only concern was finding a way to alleviate the pain.

Charles sent his son out of the room. He pushed the cedar chest out at the foot of the bed, giving himself a space between it and the bed. He instructed Rose to move down towards him. She looked at Rachael for her approval. Rachael smiled and helped her, holding her shoulders while she scooted her body towards Charles. Rachael wiped Rose's face and kissed her on her forehead. Trying to put Rose at ease, Charles assured her everything would be alright. He pushed her legs apart to examine her. He told Rachael he could see the baby's head. Rachael bent down to get clean towels from the cedar chest. She wanted to prepare things so she could clean the baby once it entered the world. When Rachael stood up, Charles was cutting the umbilical cord of a healthy baby boy.

Charlie was downstairs, pacing back and forth from the living room to the kitchen. Finally, he heard a baby's cry. Moments later, he heard Rose scream. Fear gripped his heart. He wondered what was wrong. Why was she screaming? He ran upstairs and stood at the bedroom door. As he reached for the doorknob, he heard his father yelling,

"Rachael put the baby down and come quick."

Charlie froze and prayed *God, please let Rose be alright. Don't take her from me.* Just as he finished his prayer, Rose let out another blood-curdling scream.

Rose's scream was intertwined with Rachael's shriek, "Oh, my God! My God!"

Then everything was quiet. Charlie's knees felt like water. He crumbled to the floor. He was still kneeling when his father emerged out of the bedroom with his bag. "Congratulations, son, you have a baby boy...."

Charlie stood to his feet when he heard the words *baby boy*. Breathing as if he had just run a race, he grabbed his father's hand, and words rapidly tumbled out of his mouth, "Thank you, Dad. How is Rose? Is the baby alright?"

"Calm down, son. Rose is fine. She is a trooper. You didn't let me finish."

Bracing himself, he looked at his father with fear, "Is there something wrong with the baby?"

Charles could see and hear his son's anxiety. He disapproved of Charlie's relationship with Rose but knew his son loved her and he seemed to be happy. He remembered when he was happy. *He met Charlie's mother, Margaret, at a country club cotillion. He thought she was the prettiest girl in the room. When he asked her to dance, she smiled and placed her hand in his. They dated for a year. Her parents were old money, and so were his, so they approved when Charles asked Margaret to be his wife. The wedding was elaborate. When Margaret told him she was pregnant, he was the happiest man in the world. Margaret had three miscarriages before having Charlie. He remembered the pain after the loss of each baby. Charles and Margaret felt he was God's gift when Charlie was born. Their goal was to make sure their miracle baby had the best life they had to offer. Now his miracle child was a father of twins, and the mother of his grandchildren was a colored woman.*

"Sir, is something wrong with the baby?"

"No. The babies are fine."

Charlie stood with his mouth open.

"Shut your mouth, son! You're in for many sleepless nights."

Charlie took a deep breath and asked, "Sir, did you say babies?"

"Yes, twins. A boy and a girl. Do you know what you're going to name them?"

Charlie stood staring into his father's face. After a moment, he said, "We said if we had a boy, we would name him Robert, after your father. Sarah was the name we liked for a girl, after Rose's grandmother. Twins?"

Trying to sound indifferent, "Well if those are the names, little Robert and Sarah are healthy. Rachael is cleaning them up a bit. She will let you know when you can see your family." Charlie walked his father down the stairs. He held his father's coat. Dr. Blair slid his arms into his coat and left.

Charlie stood holding the doorknob; he thought about his father's words *see your family.* He knew it took a lot for his father to say those words.

Rachael stepped out of the bedroom and called downstairs, "Your twins want to meet their father."

CHAPTER THIRTEEN

Rose and Charlie

Upon seeing their baby for the first time, most mothers feel joy. When Rose saw her twins, she was shocked. There was a feeling of bewilderment. She felt God was playing a cruel joke. Charlie stood by the bed, looking down at his twins in disbelief.

Charlie gently picked up his daughter. He sat in a chair beside the bed, holding Sarah, while Rose held Robert to her breast. During Rose's pregnancy, Rose nor Charlie ever spoke about who they thought the baby would resemble. If either thought about it, it was never given voice. Now they had twins. One pink and the other beige. Charlie looked down at Sarah snuggled in the fold of his arm. He smiled. Then he looked over at Robert suckling on Rose's breast. He and Rose looked at one another with tears in their eyes. At that moment, nothing else mattered to them.

"Rose, they are beautiful."

She looked at him. Tears of joy streamed down her face. "They are my babies."

Robert held Sarah up. He kissed her gently on her head. "Our babies," he responded.

At that moment, Rose vowed to herself she would do whatever it took to make sure her babies would have the best possible life, no matter the cost.

CHAPTER FOURTEEN

Rose

Even though happiness occupied every crevice of Rose's home, sadness had a way of pushing its way into her house. Rose sat on the side of the bed, exhausted. Sleeplessness had been her constant companion since the birth of the twins. They woke up every two to three hours demanding to be fed. When she wasn't awakened by the twins, her sleep was disturbed by a reoccurring dream that troubled her. Tonight, it was the dream, not the twins.

The moon played hide-and-seek behind the clouds causing a faint streak of light to filter through the curtains. The trees outside her bedroom window swayed in the wind. Rose sat on the side of the bed and watched the shadows made by the trees dance on their bedroom wall. As she eased herself off the edge of the bed, Charlie moaned and turned over. She glanced at him over her shoulder and then turned around, so she could see his face. She watched him sleeping peacefully; she desired a peaceful night's sleep. A feeling of envy washed over her, but she knew Charlie was doing all he could to make things easy for her. She couldn't believe this man loved her enough to defy his family and that he was the father of her babies.

Receiving help from her mother wasn't an option because her mother's baby was due any day. She couldn't wait to introduce her mother to her twin grandbabies. Rose's mother had not always approved of Rose's choices, but she was always there for her. Her Aunt Rachael dropped by twice a day, early morning, and late evening, to help Rose with the twins.

* * *

On February 7, Rose's mother gave birth to Rose's baby brother, James. On February 10, Rachael knocked on Rose's door, but this was not her usual late-evening visit to help Rose with the twins. When Charlie answered the door, he hugged her. He was puzzled because her hug lingered longer and harder than usual. When she finally released her arms from around his body, she continued clinging to his arms. Rachael had grown to like Charlie. She spoke with him privately in the hallway. They stood for a moment, locked in a stare. Charlie took Rachael's hands in his. He exhaled deeply, releasing his breath and letting go of Rachael's hand. She followed him into the living room, where Rose sat on the sofa with Sarah in her arms. Charlie kissed Rose on her forehead and took Sarah. He brought Sarah to Rachael and leaned over so Rachael could kiss her goodnight. He then left the room, leaving Rose and Rachael alone momentarily. Rachael watched Charlie as he left, holding Sarah in his arms. She cleared her throat before asking, "Is Robert sleeping?"

Rose smiled. "Yes. He is such a good baby. They both are."

"They are changing every day."

"Yes, they are. I never thought I could love anyone as much as I love these two babies."

Rose could see from her Aunt Rachael's face something was not right. Just as Rose was about to ask Rachael what was bothering her, Charlie came back to the living room without Sarah. Rachael was sitting on the piano bench. He sat beside Rose on the sofa.

Rachael knew there was no good way to say what she had to say, so she just let the words tumble from her lips, "Rose, my sister, your mother is dead."

Charlie took Rose's hand in his. She didn't move.

Rachael took a deep breath and continued, "Her womb was perforated. They couldn't stop the bleeding."

Rose said nothing. She sat gazing at her aunt. Rachael raised herself from the bench. Charlie stood up immediately. Rachael looked at him and shook her head. He understood her gesture, and he sat back down beside Rose. Rachael left.

Without saying a word, Rose got up from the sofa. Charlie watched her as she walked into the kitchen. He followed her but wanted to give her space, so he stood at the kitchen door. Silence hung in the house like a thick fog. Charlie felt helpless. He wanted to comfort her but didn't know what to do.

Rose went to the sink and started washing the babies' bottles. Rachael's words, *your mother is dead,* echoed in her head. The silence was broken by a scream erupting like a volcano from Rose's gut. She suddenly turned and threw a baby bottle across the kitchen. It hit the Frigidaire and shattered. She crumbled to the floor sobbing. Charlie went to her and tried to hold her in his arms, but she pushed him away. He sat on the floor not far from her. Rose had seven-day-old twins and no mother to give her love and motherly advice. She was utterly devastated and broken-hearted and her tears flowed uncontrollably for two hours. When she finally spoke, she told Charlie she hadn't been sleeping because she had dreamt about her mother for the last three nights. In her dream, her mother was dressed in all white. Her face was glowing. Through her tears, Rose told Charlie her mother looked at her with a beautiful smile and said *my grandbabies are beautiful.* Rose said she asked her mother *how could you know because you haven't seen them?* She said her mother just smiled and said *I have seen them. Don't be sad. Please remember what appears to be greener pastures are not always better pastures. I love you. Take care of my grandbabies.* Then she just disappeared. Rose told Charlie she woke up every time with a sinking feeling in the pit of her stomach.

Charlie embraced her and said, "Please don't shut me out. Let me help you through this." They sat on the floor in each other's arms.

Shaking her head in disbelief, Rose said, "Mama came to see me almost every week after she learned I was pregnant. She let me know that she wasn't happy I was pregnant. She knew I was scared. We would sit and talk about the baby and what labor would be like. We talked about everything. We would laugh because sometimes our babies would kick at the same time. We laughed because my baby would be older than his uncle or aunt. Charlie, she was my best friend." Rose started to cry again. Charlie rocked her in his arms. They sat there in silence. Rose felt safe.

A week later, Rose sat with her family during the funeral service. Charlie was by her side. Robert squirmed in her arms while Sarah slept in Charlie's arms. Her brothers and sisters made over their niece and nephew. Rose's family commented Sarah looked like Rose and Robert looked like his father. Friends of the family gave polite phony smiles to Rose and Charlie and raised eyebrows at the twins. Rose saw her brother, James, for the first time. He looked like their mother. Her father never looked at her in the church or graveside. Tears streamed down her face because she had lost her mother and no longer had a father. She needed him. She needed to be able to visit her father so she could get to know her baby brother, but she didn't know if that would ever be possible. Without a relationship with her father, her children would never know a grandparent. Charlie's father delivered his grandchildren but hadn't seen them since.

CHAPTER FIFTEEN

Rose

Her mother's death left an emptiness – a hole in her soul that Charlie nor the twins could fill; but her mother's death gave her a strength, a resilience, and a determination she never realized she had. Rose had learned what unconditional love of a mother was when she told her mother she was pregnant. She knew that was the kind of love she would have for Robert and Sarah.

Rachael tried to fill in as a mother and Rose appreciated Rachael being an anchor for her. Rachael brought James to Lynchburg under the pretense of taking him shopping or attending church with her. Through stolen moments, Rose and her twins were able to have a relationship with James. As the children grew older, the twins and James became best friends; in fact, he was more like their brother.

    Rose loved telling James stories about their mother. She told him when their mother was pregnant with him, she was pregnant with his niece and nephew. She told him about times when her mother would visit her, and they would stand facing each other, rubbing their bellies against one another, and burst into laughter. She told him they were like two best friends pregnant with children and that they wanted their children to know one another. James repeatedly heard how excited their mother was about having him. She told him their mother knew she was having a little boy, and she knew she was naming him James because there was a James in the Bible who was a servant of God. Rose told James their mother's prayer was he would be a servant of God. The memories she shared with her brother brought her moments of joy and laughter.

    Despite her relationship with her father, Rose wanted James to know their mother the way she knew her.

CHAPTER SIXTEEN

Charlie

September 1936. Love and pain walked hand in hand through her life. The morning had been quiet. Rose looked forward to the weekend because Charlie was home to help with the twins. Saturday morning started with Sarah jumping in bed with her parents. She was only there for a few minutes before Robert came in to join them. Rolling over, Charlie kissed Rose. The twins giggled. Rose loved those moments. Those were the moments when they were the only people in the world. Charlie wrestled with Sarah and Robert before he got up to dress and make breakfast for them.

Rose changed the twins from their pajamas into some play clothes. They went to the kitchen for breakfast. Rose got the twins settled at the table where Charlie had two bowls of cereal and two glasses of milk waiting.

Not happy with his milk, Robert looked at Rose and said, "Water, I want water."

Rose got a glass from the cabinet and went to the sink to get Robert some water. Through the window above the sink, Rose saw Charlie sitting in the backyard under the pear tree. A brisk wind was blowing. The leaves falling from the pear tree resembled ballerinas as they whirled in the wind and fell to the ground around Charlie. He appeared to be reading a letter. He laid the paper on the ground. Even from the kitchen window, she could see fear in his eyes. She wondered *what he was reading*. He closed his eyes for a moment as though he might be praying. His body appeared to jerk. Rose opened the kitchen door. Jarred by the sound of the door, Charlie quickly picked the paper up and crammed it into his jacket pocket. He stood and walked towards Rose. He stopped in front of her and gave her a gentle kiss. She could feel his body trembling.

"Charlie, what's wrong? You're trembling."

"Nothing. Just a little chill from the wind."

"Are you feeling sick?"

He smiled and gently stroked her face. "I feel fine. My Rose, I love you." He kissed her again before going inside to play with his children.

CHAPTER SEVENTEEN

The Twins

Rose and Charlie's twins had been the subject of neighborhood gossip since their birth. When Robert was born, Charlie's father handed him to Rachael, and she counted his fingers and toes and examined the coloration around his ears and fingers. Then she leaned over and whispered to Rose *it's a boy, and he's white*. A few minutes later, instead of the afterbirth expelling, Charles told Rose he saw the head of another baby. Through all her pain, Rose remembered herself whispering *twins*. She also remembered Charles saying *Push hard! Here it comes*. When Sarah made her way into the world, Charles regarded her with a perplexed expression, and handed her over to Rachael, who looked at her ears and fingers, and screamed, "*Oh my God!*" When Rose asked what was wrong, Rachael answered, "*It's a girl. She's colored*!"

The word spread through the neighborhood that Rose had given birth to twins. When the neighbors saw the babies, they were shocked. They made jokes and laughed behind Rose's back. When Rose took them out, people never doubted Sarah was her child. When they saw Robert, they wanted to know if she was his nanny. She hadn't been able to find the words to explain to Charlie the hurt she felt when people talked about her children.

Her children were different. Rose knew in time; they would know they were different. One Saturday evening, after Rose had given the twins their evening bath and washed their hair, she sat on the sofa. She told Sarah to get the comb, brush, and hair grease. Sarah flopped on the floor between her mother's legs. As Rose towel-dried her daughter's hair, Sarah stroked the hair on her mother's legs. Rose parted Sarah's wavy, kinky hair, rubbing dollops of grease in her scalp. Robert sat watching. When Rose was not looking, he put his little hand in the container of Royal Crown.

"Look, Mommy, I am doing my hair like you are doing Sarah's."

"Lord, have mercy, Robert." Rose looked at her son, shining as bright as a sixty-watt light bulb from the grease he had rubbed on his face and across the front half of his head. His hair was slicked down. "Robert, baby, you don't need grease in your hair."

Looking a bit puzzled, Robert asked, "Why not? You're putting it in Sarah's hair."

"I know, son, but you don't need it. You get a haircut. You take a different kind of care of your hair." Rose did not know what else to say to her son. She did not want to say that you have hair like your father, who is white, and your sister has hair closer to your colored mother. She looked at her son, whose face looked like the morning sun, and said, "You just don't need it."

Robert retorted, "I know why I don't need it! It's because I'm a boy, and Sarah is a girl."

Rose looked at him and smiled, "You are right, my son. You are right. Now I'm going to have to give you another bath and wash your hair again."

From the first day Robert and Sarah started school, they dealt with their differences with comments like, *you are twins? Chocolate and vanilla. We won't have a problem telling you apart.* They heard these comments from their classmates and some of their teachers. Charlie couldn't understand the hatred. He loved both of his children and wanted them to be happy. Even though he knew schools were segregated, he spoke with Rose about moving Robert to another school, one where the students were white. Rose wouldn't entertain the idea. She would not have her son posing as though he was white. Besides, she didn't want to separate the twins. How would she explain the separation to Sarah?

CHAPTER EIGHTEEN

Rose

October 1940. Time doesn't heal all wounds. Nine years had passed since Rose's mother died. The children were getting older and more independent, and Rose missed their demands for her attention. It was Saturday, and everyone had plans except Rose. The twins were with their Aunt Rachael and their Uncle James. James was now living in Lynchburg with Rachael. Selling bootleg whiskey and raising a child weren't compatible, so Rachael got a job as a cook in the Lantern Tea Room in downtown Lynchburg. The twins and James were excited about their Aunt Rachael's new job. Whenever they wanted apple pie, they would go through the back door of the tearoom to visit Rachael while she was working.

Today Charlie was checking on some rental properties, which meant Rose was alone. She walked through the house looking for something to do. She stood in front of the piano momentarily, staring down at the keys. Without purpose, she ran her fingers over them. Desiring a second cup of coffee, she went to the kitchen, got a cup from the cupboard, and she poured herself a half cup of coffee. Feeling lost and useless, she opened the kitchen door, sat at the kitchen table, and watched birds flitting around the pear tree. She didn't know when she stopped watching the birds but suddenly, she realized she was staring into a lukewarm cup of coffee and tears were slipping from her eyes, falling into her cup. She wiped her tears with her thumb. Silence was Rose's enemy when she was alone in the house because silence permitted pain to sneak in, bringing with it tears.

Her mother's death left a deep hole in her spirit. Her father refused to acknowledge her as his daughter since she had decided to cohabitate with the "enemy" was more painful than she could have imagined. She often looked at Charlie, Sarah, and Robert and questioned how her loving them could cause her so much pain. She often wondered if her father missed her as much as she missed him. *How could he act like I don't exist? I could never imagine doing that to a child of mine.* Rose's siblings told her their father hadn't uttered her name since their mother's death. Cupping her face in her hands, she held her hands over her nose and mouth to muffle the sounds trying to erupt from her soul. He had to know how much she loved him. *I was his shadow.* Through her tears, she smiled. *If he chopped wood, I wanted to chop wood. If he worked in the garden, I would want to work in the garden. He taught me how to put a worm on a fishing hook, how to cast my line, and how to patiently wait. We would spend all day on the bank of the James River, enjoying being together. I want my children to experience times like I had with their grandddad.* Her eyes again filled with tears. *I don't understand. God, I don't understand. What can I do to make things right between us? My children have no one to call granddad.*

The front door opened and slammed close. The twins yelled, "Mom, we're home. Where are you?"

Rose pushed herself from the table. Wiping her face, she smiled. "I'm in the kitchen." She was happy for the noise.

CHAPTER NINTEEN

Rose

December 1940. The world was crumbling and falling like grains of sand in an hourglass. It was a quiet Saturday morning, and Rose sat at the kitchen table enjoying a leisurely cup of coffee. Taking a deep breath and letting it out, she smiled. There was nothing like enjoying the aroma of coffee, especially on a winter morning. Charlie and the twins were out shopping for a Christmas tree. Rose drank the last bit of her coffee and pushed herself from the table. She walked through the house; everything was clean and in place. Looking around the living room for a spot for the tree, she laughed out loud and asked herself, *"Why are you doing this, Rose? You know the tree will go where it always goes, in front of the window across from the piano."*

Rose walked over to the window and pulled back the curtain. The trees in the front yard were bare, the morning was gray, and snow flurries danced in the air. A few of the neighbors were bustling about the neighborhood. A low-hanging gray cloud looking like an angel made her smile. *Mama, is that you?* She stood watching the angel cloud as it slowly changed its formation. When the angel cloud disappeared, a red cardinal perched on a limb of one of the trees in front of the house. She covered her mouth in adulation. She whispered, "A red cardinal, an angel is nearby. Mama, it is you, isn't it? If you are near, I know my prayers will be heard. Lord, am I asking too much to ask that somehow there will be a coming together of families? My daddy has two beautiful grandchildren he doesn't know. Father God, tell me how to make things right. I need my daddy. How can I make my daddy see Charlie is a good man? I hear the gossip. I see the looks, Lord. Were we wrong to love one another?"

Just as she was about to return to the kitchen for a second cup of coffee, she was startled by banging on the front door.

Rose yelled, "Who is it?"

"It's me, Rachael. Open the door."

When she opened the door, Rachael stood there with tears streaming down her face.

"Aunt Rachael, what's wrong?"

"It's your father!"

"Daddy? What's wrong?"

"Rose, he's dead. He had a massive heart attack."

Rose turned and walked into the living room. Rachael closed the door and followed behind her.

"Rose, did you hear what I said?"

"Yes, I heard you." Turning to face her aunt, "How could he die without ever getting to know his grandchildren?"

Rachael whispered sadly, "I don't know."

Rose didn't know whether to be angry or sad. Why had God let her father die before they had a chance to make amends? "He never gave me a chance to be his little girl again. Aunt Rachael, he never gave me a chance to...."

With open arms, Rachael walked to Rose, embracing her. Rose cried. Enormous sadness, accompanied by anger, had once again invaded her world.

Christmas came and went. Rose only left the house to attend her father's funeral. She had a sudden urge to clean the house from top to bottom. She felt like cleaning would make things better.

CHAPTER TWENTY

Rose

October 19, 1945. The sky had collapsed. It wasn't supposed to fall, but it did. Rose was feeling a bit strange. She wasn't sick, but she didn't feel well. One minute she felt like someone was having a tug-of-war match in her stomach, but the next minute she felt like butterflies were fluttering in it. Deciding a cup of ginger tea might be good, she got ginger and a cup from the cupboard. Then she measured out a teaspoon of ginger and put it in her cup along with some of the hot water she had heating on the stove. She sat at her kitchen table trying to enjoy her tea and the quietness of the morning, but she couldn't shake the nagging feeling in the pit of her stomach. She thought the tea would calm the fluttering feeling, but so far, it wasn't working.

Charlie was at work. The twins were at school. A sudden clap of thunder startled Rose. She pushed herself from the table and went to the window. When she pulled the curtain back, a bluish-yellow streak of lightning danced across the sky. The sight of the lightning flashing intensified the feeling in her stomach. *Why am I feeling like this? Robert didn't want to go to school today. Maybe I should have let him stay at home.* She sipped her tea as she listened to the rain hitting the roof. Her thoughts were interrupted by another loud clap of thunder and a sudden downpour of rain. She wrapped her arms around herself. *Thunder and lightning in October, some would say this is a sign of the last days.* She sat back in her chair at the table. She thought *I need to start attending church again.* She could count the times on her hands she had been inside a church since she and Charlie had been together.

The rain dancing on the roof stopped as quickly as it started. She got up and went back to the window. The sun was starting to peek through the clouds. She was glad to see the sun. *Maybe some fresh air will help me to shake this feeling,* she thought. She picked up her cup of tea and headed for the front door. When she opened it, she mumbled, "*Indian Summer*". She stood in the door watching as her neighbors left their houses with lunch pails and brown bags. Bessie, her next-door neighbor, stood on her porch with a broom in her hands. She smiled and waved. Rose waved back.

A cat, in the Fuquas' yard, caught Rose's attention. She watched as the cat crouched low in the grass. It crept quietly towards a bird pecking for food. Rose held her breath. Just as the cat sprung, the bird flew into a tree. Rose exhaled. She realized her stomach felt better. *Why did I watch?* She asked. *Why didn't I yell to warn the bird?* Rose smiled. She was happy the bird was going to live to see another day. The cat reminded her of her neighbors, sneaky and ready to pounce.

She took a deep breath, inhaled the fresh morning air, and went back into the house. She put her cup in the sink and started to wash dishes, but she found herself staring at the sky out of the kitchen window. She was suddenly overcome with sadness and tears ran down her face. *Mama, the twins need you and I need you. You were so right when you told me love wasn't always enough. How did you know? Did you have times with Daddy when loving him wasn't enough? Mama, our love got us through the gossip of the neighbors. And it got us through family turning their backs on us. I thought the love Charlie and I have for each other would get us through anything. Maybe it would have if we didn't have the twins.* She felt bad for having that thought. *Mama, some people even question whether they're twins. Love is not enough to keep them safe, especially Robert. It hurts me to see how angry and sad he is sometimes. It seems as though people want to punish him for being who he is. Sarah is a good sister. She will fight to the end for him. Charlie doesn't understand just because his love is blind for me doesn't mean the community's love for his children is blind. Sometimes I think the twins resent us because of the hatred they feel from outside this house. I feel they blame us. And I guess we are to blame. If we had just stayed with our…, you were right, Mama. The twins come to me, but I don't know how to fix things for Robert. It's so hard to talk to Charlie about this, so we don't talk. He said he would always be here for me, and he has been true to his word. He could have walked away, but he didn't. Mama, I still believe he loves me. I know he loves his children, but then I ask myself, can you love what you don't know or understand? Mama, I miss you! I need you!* A knock on the door pulled Rose away from the window and her internal conversation with her mother. It was Rachael with a bushel of green beans.

"Hi, Aunt Rachael."

"Hey, I would give you a hug." Holding up a bushel basket, "Look at what Mrs. Fears gave me."

Rose ran her fingers through the bushel basket of green beans. "How do you like working at the Lantern Tea Room?"

"I have no complaints. Look, James and I don't need all of these beans."

Rose laughs, "Come on in." Together they took the basket to the kitchen. "Do you want a cup of coffee?"

"Yes, if it's no trouble."

"Not at all." Rose took a cup from the cupboard. She poured coffee from the coffee pot sitting on the back of the stove. "It's strong. Do you want sugar or milk?"

"No thanks."

Sitting with both elbows on the table and both hands holding the cup, Rachael slurped the coffee. "This is perfect."

"Good. Enjoy your coffee while I get us two large bowls." Taking two bowls from the cupboard, Rose handed one to Rachael. "Here you go."

Rachael got up, took the bowl, sat back in her chair, slightly opened her legs, and placed the bowl between them. Rose took a seat and went through the same motions. In silence, they snapped the tips off the beans, placing the tips in a small bowl Rose had placed on the table and the beans in the large bowls they had placed in their laps.

When Rose's bowl was full, she took it to the sink to wash the beans in her bowl. After washing the beans, she dumped them in a pan she had placed on the table and started working on snapping a second bowl of beans. Not looking up, Rose said, "Aunt Rachael, I miss Mama."

Rachael responded with a sad smile, "I do too."

"I miss Daddy too. I wish he had forgiven me."

"Baby, I think he did. He loved you. I think you were his favorite. It would've been hard for him to lose you to any man, but a white man made it harder." Not another word was said. Rose and Rachael spent the morning snapping and canning green beans.

CHAPTER TWENTY-ONE

Charlie

When the twins came home, they found Rose in the kitchen putting mason jars of green beans in the pantry. They kissed her and were off to their rooms. No complaints. They had an uneventful day. Rose busied herself in the kitchen preparing Charlie's favorite foods – meatloaf, mashed potatoes, peas, and hot rolls. Before her Aunt Rachael came with the green beans, her plan was to make a chocolate cake, but since time did not permit, she decided to make fried apple pies. Charlie loved her fried apple pies. She was looking forward to a relaxing evening with her husband. She hadn't had one in a while. *We will all be okay,* she thought.

She was putting plates on the table when she heard Charlie's car. Sarah and Robert ran downstairs to greet their father when he walked through the door. Even though this was an everyday ritual for the twins, they were giddy with excitement.

Charlie pulled up and parked his car in front of their special place. He leaned over the driver's seat to get a rose and packages from the car's back seat. When he got out, he placed everything on the car's roof. Then he locked the car. He smiled as he thought about being greeted at the door by Rose and his children. He gathered his packages and the one rose he bought to give to the love of his life. As he started to walk away from his car, he heard a motor roaring. He turned. Headlights blinded him. He was struck. The driver didn't stop. Rose's next-door neighbor looked out the window and saw a truck speeding away. She ran out of the house screaming for Rose. When Rose ran out of her house, she saw Charlie lying in the street. She fell to her knees beside him. Caressing his head close to her breast, she screamed for someone to help her. She picked up the single rose he was still holding. He told her he loved her, and she whispered she loved him. Rose kissed him and he died in her arms. Robert and Sarah stood in the door of their parents' special place. Robert was behind his sister holding her shoulders while Sarah screamed, "Daddy, Daddy! I want my Daddy!"

CHAPTER TWENTY-TWO

Rose

Forbidden love came at a price. Death came to collect, leaving loved ones with grief, pain, and confusion. Living in a small town everyone, colored, white, and the authorities knew about Rose and Charlie. Their living together was tolerated by whites and the authorities because Charlie didn't bring her into the properties he owned in the white community. The authorities also respected his parents. Colored people felt they had no choice but to accept him in their community.

Twenty minutes after the hit and run, the police arrived. Rose was still sitting in the street holding Charlie in her arms. Rachael stood behind her trying to console Robert and Sarah. One of the police officers immediately recognized Charlie and asked another officer to go to Doctor Blair's house to inform the doctor and his wife of the situation. Even though the relationship was against the law, the police officer showed compassion to Rose and her children. After Rose and the neighbors were questioned by the authorities, Charlie's body was removed from the street.

Rachael wanted to stay by Rose's side, but Rose wanted to be alone with Sarah and Robert. Sitting between her children on the sofa, Rose put her arms around them; she could feel her children's fear creeping into her spirit. Tears ran down their faces. No one said a word. A sudden loud banging on the door startled them. Rose jumped up. Fear gripped her heart. She put her finger to her lips as a signal for the twins to be quiet. Immediately Robert grabbed Sarah by the hand and led her to the space between the piano and the wall. At school, Sarah had been Robert's protector, but tonight Robert was being the protective big brother. Rose approached the front door with caution. When she opened it, Margaret and Charles Blair were standing there. The redness in her eyes and the scowl on Margaret's face were a depiction of hatred. Margaret pushed her way in past Rose screaming, "You nigger bitch! My son is dead because of you! You killed my son!"

Rose was cognizant of Margaret's anguish, but she was grappling with her own pain. She refused to be treated like she didn't matter. Meeting Margaret's gaze she coldly whispered, "I told you once, I am not a nigger, and I am not a bitch. I would advise you to leave before we are both sorry."

Charles tried to grab Margaret's arm, but she pushed him away. Neighbors had come out of their houses. Some were on their porches and others were standing in the street in front of Rose's house watching. Charles closed the door.

Angry and horrified, Rose looked toward where the twins were hiding. She could see Robert peeking around the living room door. She waved him back. He obediently retreated with his sister between the piano and the wall. Margaret charged towards Rose forcing her to walk backwards into the living room. Again, Charles tried to hold Margaret's arm, but she broke away from his grip and put her finger in Rose's face. When she did, Robert abruptly sprang from the side of the piano and positioned himself in front of his mother, prompting Margaret to become immobile as if in a catatonic state. Charles observed Robert and noticed the cause of his wife's rage suddenly subsiding. The striking resemblance of Robert to their son was unmistakable. Margaret's intention when she pushed her way into Rose's house was to strip Rose down to her bare soul. Instead, Margaret was crumbling to the floor sobbing uncontrollably. Charles helped his wife to the sofa. Robert embraced his mother and guided her to a beige armchair. Margaret stared across the room at Rose and Robert. Sarah eased her way to the chair where her mother sat. And like a soldier standing guard, Robert stood by his mother's chair gazing at Margaret and Charles. Staring back, Margaret's lips became a thin, almost invisible line and her eyes narrowed into slits of rage. Charles had not uttered a word. He looked at Rose and his grandchildren. He had not seen them since he had delivered the twins.

Snuggling against her mother in the chair, Sarah asked, "Mom, are you alright?"

"Yes, baby." She put her arms around Sarah to reassure her. She looked up at Robert who was still standing like a soldier staring at the grandparents he had never met. Rose reached for his arm. He broke his gaze to look at his mother. "Robert, Sarah, please go to your rooms." Rose could see Robert's reluctance. "I'll be alright." Sarah went down the small hallway and up the stairs to her room, but Robert situated himself at the bottom of the stairs so he could hear the conversation in the living room.

Rose wanted to scream at the Blairs to get out, but instead, she wiped her hands across her lap to stop her legs from trembling. She sat straight up in her chair and waited for the insults and accusations to come flying across the room from Margaret's mouth to slap her in her face.

Every fiber in Margaret's body wanted to tear into Rose but seeing Robert had knocked the wind out of her. She looked at Rose and said, "I don't know what he saw in you to cause him to turn his back on his family."

There was no way Rose was going to give the Blairs the pleasure of seeing her breakdown. She did not want to sit and deal with anger and accusations, but she was determined to be composed. "I think he saw the same thing in me that I saw in him, a good person. He never turned his back on you. You turned your backs on him because he chose to love me. We never talked about our color. It made a difference to you and others but not to us. Not to our children." She knew she was lying because it did make a difference to her children.

Charles, who had been sitting beside his wife with his head lowered, looked up and asked, "Can you please tell us what happened? We just need to know what happened."

Rose could see the pain etched on his face. She knew, like her, he wanted to understand what had happened. She took a deep breath and said, "I don't know. I heard a loud noise, and I ran outside. Charlie … Charlie was just lying there. That's all I know. I can't tell you any more than you have already been told by the police."

Charles opened his mouth to speak. Words trapped in his throat were choking him. Reaching for Margaret's hand, he squeezed and swallowed hard, "Did anyone see…?" He could not finish his question.

Sitting erect in her chair, her hands, one on top of the other in her lap, Rose looked at the ring on her finger. The ring Charlie had given her. She was no longer trembling. A calmness had washed over her she did not understand. She pushed herself further back in the armchair, "My neighbor was looking out the window when it happened. She said Charlie had just gathered some things from the back seat of the car and someone in a pick-up truck hit him and didn't stop. No one saw the driver."

Rose's calmness just made Margaret's venom, which had been calmed by Robert's appearance, spill over. She pulled her hand from her husband's hand, pushed herself to the edge of the sofa, and leaned forward staring into Rose's face. "How can you be so nonchalant about this? I want you to know that we will be making funeral arrangements for our son. You're not welcome at the funeral home or at the service. Am I clear?"

Keeping her composure, Rose pulled herself up out of the chair. She walked out of the living room, leaving the Blairs on the sofa. She went to the front door, opened it, and in a firm voice, she demanded, "Please leave. I want both of you out of here, now!"

Charles and Margaret entered the hallway. Margaret could not contain her emotions. Crying and pointing a finger in Rose's face, "You're the one who will be getting out. That ring on your finger means nothing. You weren't married to my son! In the eyes of the law and in my eyes, you were just his nigger whore."

Robert sprang up from the steps, pointing his finger at Margaret and then towards the door, "You heard my mother. She wants you out, so leave!"

Margaret stormed out the door. Walking out behind his wife with his head lowered, Charles stopped and looked at Rose as though he wanted to say something. She could see his eyes were brimming with tears. Just as he as was about to speak, Margaret screamed, "Charles, come on!"

Closing the door, Rose leaned against it. Robert looked at his mother. She held up open arms, he walked into her embrace, and he cried. Sarah stood at the top of the stairs watching and quietly whimpering, "I want my Daddy! I want my Daddy!"

CHAPTER TWENTY-THREE

Rose

Good memories were a blanket of comfort until one bad memory snatched away the covers leaving her chilled to the bone. Rose sat on the floor by the door for three hours with her children. Huddled together, they cried. They asked her questions. *Who killed our Daddy? Why did someone kill our Daddy? Why didn't the driver stop? Was it done on purpose? Why did their daddy's mother think you killed him? Why does she hate us? Why didn't their Daddy's father say something?* Rose had no answers she wanted to share with her children.

Rose felt a wave of appreciation wash over her when the twins decided to retire to their rooms. The silence that ensued was almost deafening. She switched off the lights in the living room before taking a seat on the sofa. Charlie's presence was keenly felt, a comforting presence that permeated the air around her.

Happy moments flooded her mind. She closed her eyes and thought about the day they moved into their special place. She put on a white dress the first night in their special place. Her hair framed her face and lay on her shoulders. She and Charlie stood in their backyard under the pear tree. Fireflies danced around them. The sky was filled with stars, and the light of a full moon illuminated their special moment. Charlie took her hands in his and lifted them upward towards the heavens. They vowed to God that they would be faithful to each other. Charlie took a ring out of his pocket and placed it on the ring finger of her left hand. He pulled her to him and gently kissed her. It did not matter what the law or Margaret thought; at that moment, they vowed to themselves and God that they were husband and wife.

When she opened her eyes, it felt like a dam had burst, and through her tears, she saw the single rose on the coffee table. Her hands trembled with grief. For fourteen years, Charlie had brought her a daily rose. She lifted the rose to her lips, and there sat Charlie, smiling back at her from the beige chair.

Suddenly a strange feeling came over her. She felt like she had forgotten something. What was it? Why couldn't she remember? The memory quivered annoyingly on the edge of her consciousness. Her eyes searched the room's darkness, trying to shake the feeling. She wanted sleep to come and take away all the pain. She closed her eyes, hoping to force rest to invade her consciousness. *Charlie, what am I going to do without you? Where are we going to live? I know your parents are going to put us out of here.* She closed her eyes and started to pray. *Father, I need your help. I don't know where to go or what to do. I have no one to turn to anymore. I have tried to be strong. It's getting harder and harder. God, I don't understand why you have taken so much from me, but I am still trusting you. Amen.*

Tears continued to stream down her face in the dark stillness of the room. She got up and made her way up the stairs to their bedroom, where she stretched out on the bed. Envisioning Charlie's arms around her, she felt herself slipping into slumber.

Suddenly, she found herself struggling to breathe. Bolting upright in the bed, she gasped for air. Her eyes opened wide, gazing through the darkness as words from the past ricocheted off her bedroom walls: *she needs to be careful. Tell her to stay out of the line of fire.* She was trembling, but she was not cold. *No! Why am I remembering that? That was more than fourteen years ago*, she thought. "Fourteen years ago," she mumbled out loud to herself.

A Mother's White Lie

CHAPTER TWENTY-FOUR

Rose

Love was her protection. On the day of Charlie's funeral, the sky was gray, and rain poured from the heavens. It was as though the angels were crying with Rose and her children as they stood in the rain across the street from the white church where Charlie's service was being held. With a somber demeanor, they maintained their vigil until the coffin was taken from the church and transferred to the hearse. They whispered their final goodbyes as the hearse departed the church for the graveyard. The pain Rose felt was akin to a knife plunging into her heart shredding it into pieces, further exacerbating her existing emotional trauma.

Two weeks had passed since Charlie's funeral. Uncertainty was her constant companion. Rose dreaded opening her eyes each morning because with the start of each day came the fear of whether this was the day she and the twins would have no place to live.

Three days after Charlie's funeral, Rose received a letter from the law offices of Howard Berg and Associates requesting her presence at a meeting in their office. It had been on her coffee table since she took it from her mailbox. She sat staring at the letter like it was a snake waiting to strike. With trembling hands, she picked it up and held it to her chest. Fear was squeezing her heart, causing it to beat wildly. She heard Sarah and Robert laughing. They were in the kitchen making sandwiches. She took the letter out of the envelope and read it three times. *What could they want?* Then she remembered the last thing Margaret said to her the night Charlie was killed. *'You are the one who will be getting out.' Was Margaret making good on her promise? Even though our special place belonged to Charlie, I am sure his parents will now have control of all of Charlie's properties. Where am I going to go with my children?*

On the morning of the appointment, she convinced herself she had to go because she needed to know what was about to happen to her and her children. She remembered her Aunt Rachael telling her she was always welcomed in her home. A long hot bath relaxed the tension she was feeling. She put on a loose-fitting straight black dress with long sleeves and a single strand of pearls. She looked in the mirror at her hair, brushed it back, and put it in a chignon bun. She did not try to cover the dark circles around her eyes from sleepless nights since Charlie's death. Her only make-up was pink lipstick.

When Rose arrived at the law offices of Howard Berg and Associates, the receptionist, a blond girl wearing a tight blue sweater and ruby red lipstick, greeted her and led her to the conference room, where she offered Rose a seat at the end of a long oak table. Rose's stomach was in knots because everything in her told her that she and her children would be without a home at the end of the meeting.

Howard Berg, a tall, slightly balding man with a ruddy complexion, who looked to be about sixty years old, walked into the conference room. After placing a folder on the table, he introduced himself to Rose. "Miss Franklin, are you alright?"

She was so focused on the folder that she didn't see him offering his hand for her to shake. "Yes."

His handshake was firm. Her hand was sweaty. Attorney Berg took a seat near Rose at the head of the table.

When he was seated, the receptionist announced, "Dr. and Mrs. Charles Blair are here. Attorney Berg, would you like me to bring them in?"

"Yes, please."

When Margaret entered the room, Attorney Berg stood. He shook Charles's hand and then Margaret's hand.

"Please, have a seat, Dr. and Mrs. Blair."

Charles pulled out a chair for Margaret, and he sat in the chair beside her. Margaret and Charles sat across the table from Rose but didn't acknowledge her. Rose, seeing them knew the inevitable was about to happen. *They are acting like I am invisible. Let's see how long that lasts. No matter what, stay composed,* she told herself.

Attorney Berg looked at Rose and nodded. Rose looked at him and thought *he would be great at playing poker. His face shows nothing.* Then he turned to the Blairs and said, "Thank you for coming. You are here for the reading of the last will and testament of Charles William Blair, Jr. I…."

Refusing to look at Rose, but pointing her finger across the table, Margaret interrupted Attorney Berg with, "Why is *that* here?" Charles reached over to Margaret. She jerked away. "Don't touch me. I want an answer! What the hell is that nigger whore doing here?"

Rose wanted to run, but her legs felt like lead. *Breathe*, she commanded herself. After taking a deep breath, she felt a calmness wash over her. She noticed Margaret wouldn't look at her. Rose couldn't help but wonder if Margaret's hatred and anger for her were overriding her grief for her son. Charles did make eye contact, but then he lowered his head. *Now ain't that something,* Rose thought. *I'm looking him in the eye, and he is looking away from me like I'm white and he's colored.*

Attorney Berg turned to Margaret. His face was stoic. "Mrs. Blair let's be civil. The three of you are here at your son's request. Like I said before I was interrupted, you've been asked here for the reading of Charles William Blair, Jr.'s last will and testament. I'll only read the parts of this document that directly affect all of those present at this meeting. But before I do that, I'll read this letter Charlie requested to have read before the reading of his will."

"Wait!" Margaret commanded. "When did Charlie have this will drawn up?"

Attorney Berg sat for a moment without saying a word. When he spoke, he looked directly at Margaret and said, "In 1931, when he moved in with Rose."

"My son wouldn't do that!"

Attorney Berg responded, "But he did, Mrs. Blair."

"Why? Why would he do that?"

"Mrs. Blair, please be patient and your questions will be answered."

Rose tried to prepare her mind and heart for whatever was about to happen. Looking across the table at Margaret, Rose could see Margaret's face had turned beet red, and her eyes were pools of bitterness and hatred. Margaret had gone from not making eye contact with Rose to staring at her. Rose was not going to be intimidated by Margaret's scowling stare. Rose took a deep breath and held it for a moment. She quietly exhaled and braced herself.

Attorney Berg looked at the Blairs and then at Rose. He began reading the letter.

Dear Mom, Dad, and Rose,

Mom, I love you. I know you wanted what you thought was best for me. I found what I needed and what was best for me when I found Rose. I wish you knew her the way I do. I know you would love her as much as I do if you did. Mom, she is my life. She is the air I breathe. She is the reason my heart beats. At some point, you felt that way about Dad, and he felt that way about you. I believe somewhere you lost it. Mom, you want to control everyone and everything, including Dad and me. Mom, please try to open your heart.

"Stop! Stop!" Margaret screamed. She had her hands pressed down on the table, pushing herself up. "My son didn't write that!"

Charles reached for Margaret's hand. She shoved his hand away. With open palms, Charles slammed his hands on the table.

This startled Margaret. She looked at him, "What's wrong with you?"

Not looking at her, Charles spoke through his teeth to her. "Margaret, sit down, shut up, and listen!"

"How dare you!" She retorted!

"Yes, how dare me. Sit down!" Charles commanded.

Attorney Berg waited for Charles to control the situation. Margaret reluctantly sat back in her seat. Fighting tears, she said, "Charlie had to be delusional when he wrote this. He wasn't in his right mind."

"Mrs. Blair, your son knew if he expired before you, this would be your reaction. That was his reason for writing this letter and leaving instructions that it should be read before the Last Will and Testament. I'll finish reading your son's letter, and I'm asking you to please refrain from interrupting." Looking at Charles, Attorney Berg continued reading the letter.

Dad, I love you even though I never really knew you. You were never there when I was growing up. I often wondered if it was your job or if it was because you just needed time when you were not being controlled by Mom.

Mom and Dad, please know I am of my right mind. I wanted this letter read before the reading of my Last Will and Testament because Mom, I know by this point Dad is probably having to hold you in your seat.

Rose could see Margaret was struggling to control herself. *Charlie knew his mother,* Rose thought. Even though she did not know what the will would reveal, hearing this part of the letter, Rose could not stop the smirk she felt creeping across her face. She did not want to look across the table at the Blairs but refused to be subservient, so she let her eyes roam around the room, coming to rest on the letter in Attorney Berg's hand.

After a brief pause, anticipating a reaction from Mrs. Blair, Attorney Berg cleared his throat and continued, *If I know my mom, she will want to contest it. Dad, please don't let her. I want Rose and any children we may have to have a good life.*

Rose, I love you so much. When you told me you were pregnant, I came to see Attorney Berg. No one wants to think about death, but not knowing what life has in store for me, I wanted to ensure you didn't have to worry about anything. If my mother does try to contest this will, don't worry. I have asked Attorney Berg to represent you. You don't have to worry about his fees. That has already been worked out.

I love each of you dearly.

Charlie

Rose exhaled. She did not realize she had been holding her breath. Fighting tears of gratitude, she wanted to scream but knew she had to remain calm. The letter made her feel she and her children may not be homeless.

Margaret was livid. "I don't want to sit here and listen to this."

Charles turned to his wife. "You may not want to sit here and listen, but you will. I have remained quiet for too long. Our son is dead. We both will sit here. Do you hear me? When Charlie was alive, we both failed him. I don't care if you do not want to hear it, but you will! You will sit here and listen!"

Margaret looked at Charles with the same look she had when talking to and about Rose.

Charles looked at Attorney Berg and said, "Please continue."

Attorney Berg nodded. "Now I will read Charlie's Last Will and Testament."

I, Charles William Blair, Jr., of Lynchburg, Virginia, revoke any former Wills and Codicils and declare this to be my Last Will and Testament.

Article I

Identification of Family

I am not currently married to anyone under the laws of Virginia. I am spiritually married to Rose Marie Franklin. Rose, the laws prevented us from uniting in marriage, but it will not prevent me from loving you and taking care of you after I can no longer be with you.

Rose had not wanted to cry in the presence of Margaret and Charles, but now she could not stop herself. Tears streamed down Rose's face as she listened. She searched in her pocketbook for a handkerchief. She wiped her eyes and let out an audible breath.

This was the finality for her. Attorney Berg reached over and patted her hand and continued reading.

Disposition of Property

I bequeathed all my rental properties, all funds in my bank accounts, and the contents in my safe deposit box to Rose Marie Franklin.

"That's it," said Attorney Berg as he looked at Margaret and Charles.

Margaret pushed her chair away from the table. She walked out, not saying a word. Charles got up when his wife pushed away from the table, but he sat back in his seat after she walked out.

Attorney Berg turned to Rose, "We need to schedule time for a meeting. I will give you a listing of the rental properties. I am here to give you any assistance you may need." Then he turned to Charles and asked, "Do you have questions, Mr. Blair?"

"No, I want to say something to Rose, if I may."

Attorney Berg asked Rose, "Would you like me to leave?"

"No sir, please stay."

Dr. Blair nodded his head. "That's fine. Rose, I wish I knew the right words to say to you. You made my son happy. So, I guess I want to say thank you. I should have been there for you."

"Mr. Blair, I never had a chance to thank you for being there to deliver the twins. Charlie ... well, he loved you."

"If you...."

Margaret re-entered the conference room like a whirlwind shrieking, "Charles, are you coming?" Charles left his business card on the table before leaving with Margaret.

Attorney Berg took the business card from the table and placed it before Rose. "Are you alright?"

Crying and laughing simultaneously, Rose responded, "Yes. I'm shocked. I can't believe what just happened. I feel like I am dreaming."

"Rose, you're not dreaming. Charlie loved you very much. I am here to help you with whatever you might need. We will set up another time for you to come in so we can talk about his properties and how you can handle them. I have an envelope Charlie left for you. He left instructions that I give this to you alone." He handed her a sealed envelope. "I'm going to give you some privacy. I will be back in a few minutes." He left the conference room, closing the door.

Rose sat examining the envelope before tearing it open.

September 28, 1936

Dear Rose,

I hope you never have to open this envelope. Enclosed is a note I found on my car one morning. I am sharing it with you now because I want you to be careful and look out for the twins. If you need any help with anything, Attorney Berg will help.

I love you forever.

Charlie

The second sheet of paper in the envelope looked as if it had been crumpled up and smoothed out.

The message was written in a childish scrawl.

You not wanted here! You take our jobs. You take our women right in our faces. You want to keep living? Go back to your own neighborhood or die. This is not a threat but a promise!

Gasping and placing her hands over her mouth, Rose dropped the sheets of paper on the conference table. *Had Charlie been murdered because of her?* She remembered the conversation she heard at her aunt's house. *Did someone Aunt Rachael know kill Charlie? Did Aunt Rachael know Charlie was going to be run down in front of his house? She couldn't have known. She would have said something to me.* Questions were whirling in her mind like a tornado. *Should I share this with Aunt Rachael? Are my children safe? Do I share this with anyone? I need to keep this to myself.*

Attorney Berg knocked on the conference room door before entering. He found Rose staring at the envelope she had placed back on the table in front of her.

"Are you alright, Miss Franklin?"

Taking a deep breath, she picked up the sheets of paper, put them in the envelope, and placed it on the table. Shaking her head, "Yes. I am just a bit overwhelmed." She picked the envelope up and put it in her pocketbook.

CHAPTER TWENTY-FIVE

Rose

June 17, 1949. Unfillable holes in life can produce unfulfilled desires. Sitting at the kitchen table, Rose felt like a part of her was missing. Four years had passed since Rose and the twins watched the hearse with Charlie's body pull away from the church, but the pain had not lessened. Charlie's death left a hole.

The twins had never given her any problems but raising them alone had not been easy. Even though Charlie had left them with no financial worries, Rose wanted her children to be independent. After school, Robert and his Uncle James had jobs cleaning downtown offices, and Sarah learned to cook, clean, and sew from Rose and Rachael. Sometimes on the weekends, Sarah would babysit.

The twins were good students. Rose was grateful things had changed for Robert in school. When he entered high school, girls accepted and sought after Robert for the same reason they had ridiculed him in elementary and junior high school – his white complexion and *good hair*. Sarah never had problems because she looked like all the other students in the schools they attended.

* * *

Life continued even when life had stopped. The morning air was warm and sweet; small puffy clouds were scattered about an azure sky. Polk Street was buzzing with morning activity. Mr. Madison had his horse and wagon, which contained live squawking chickens, eggs, tomatoes, green beans, squash, watermelons, cucumbers, potatoes, collard, and turnip greens waiting to be weighed and sold, parked in front of Miss Bessie's house. Rose watched as her neighbors scurried about preparing for the day.

Today was graduation day for Robert and Sarah. They were in the top ten of their graduating class. Rose's heart was filled with joy and sadness as she watched the twins receive their diplomas. She wished Charlie were there. With her hands over her heart, she thanked God.

It was also James's graduation day. Looking over at Rachael, Rose saw tears streaming down her aunt's face when James's name was called. Rose recognized that her Aunt Rachael was thinking about her sister. Rose's thoughts of her mother permeated her mind, spirit, and soul. She imagined her mother holding her hand as they watched their children step into adulthood. Tears rolled down her cheeks as she whispered softly, "I know you are watching. I hope you are proud."

They all came together at Rose's house to celebrate. The day had been filled with excitement. Family members and friends came to the house with gifts. Rose and Rachael prepared an abundance of food: baked ham, fried chicken, green beans, candied yams, chitterlings, collard greens, deviled eggs, macaroni and cheese, potato salad, corn pudding, apple cobbler, and yeast rolls. Laughter filled the house.

Rose listened as the twins, and James talked about college. James had been accepted at Howard University and Morehouse College. He wanted to be a doctor. Robert had also been accepted at Howard and Morehouse. He was unsure what he wanted to do, but he and James talked a lot about all the girls they would meet. Sarah was also accepted at Howard, Bennett College, and Spelman College. She wanted to be a teacher. Her hope was she, and Robert would attend Howard. She could not imagine being separated from her brother.

* * *

A warm breeze caused the curtains to billow inward. The moon was playing a game of hide and seek with the clouds. In bed, Sarah stared at the shadows appearing and disappearing on her bedroom walls. Looking out the window, she saw a shooting star. Smiling, she turned her face from the window. She whispered in the darkness *I wish I may. I wish I might. Have this wish I wish tonight. I wish nothing would ever separate me from my brother. Tomorrow starts our new journey.*

CHAPTER TWENTY-SIX

Sarah

If it was possible for twins to be closer than twins, Sarah and Robert were. They shared everything, or so Sarah thought. Sarah woke up excited. It was a glorious day! The sun was shining, and birds were chirping outside of her window. Sarah opened her window and inhaled deeply. The scents of Sweet Peas and Snap Dragons invaded her olfactory nerves. She smiled, twirled around the room, slid her feet into her slippers, quickly put on her bathrobe, and went to Robert's room. She knocked on the door, but he did not answer. *He's downstairs already*, she mumbled to herself. She couldn't wait to tell Robert she made a wish last night when she saw a shooting star.

The smell of eggs and bacon made her stomach growl. She was ready for breakfast as she ran into the kitchen, hugged Rose, and sat at the table. Giggling with excitement, Sarah asked, "Where is Robert?" Rose did not answer. "Mom, did you hear me? Where is Robert?"

"Child, I'm busy trying to put some breakfast on the table. I have scrambled eggs and bacon. I was about to make some pancakes. Do you want pancakes?"

"Yes, ma'am." She walked to the opened kitchen door. Again, the scents of Sweet Peas and Snapdragons invaded her nostrils. Sarah looked over her shoulder at her mother and said, "The aromas of Sweets Peas, and Snap Dragons seemed to have surrounded the house."

Rose nodded her head but said nothing.

"The scents are so intoxicating."

Rose chuckled and asked, "Little girl, what do you know about intoxication?"

"I know nothing about intoxication, Mom. The scents are just so strong this morning!" Sarah laughed and took a seat at the table, "Mom, did Robert go to Aunt Rachael's house?"

After flipping pancakes onto a plate, Rose responded, "You're full of questions this morning. Here, eat your food while it's hot." Rose placed a plate with pancakes, eggs, and bacon in front of Sarah.

Sarah extended her hand towards the syrup for her pancakes but halted mid-air upon noticing an envelope with her name on it at the center of the kitchen table. "Mom, what is that?"

Pouring herself a cup of coffee, Rose leaned against the sink. Studying her daughter, she sipped coffee and said, "I don't know. It has your name on it."

Sarah opened the envelope. She found a note from her brother.

Dear Sarah,

College is not what I want. I'm leaving. I'm not sure where I will end up. I considered joining the Army, but I'm not sure if that is for me. I love you.

Be good, and please take care of Mom.

Love you always,

Your big brother

PS: Please tell James I am sorry. I know he was also planning for all three of us to go off to college together.

Confused, Sarah sat staring at the note from her brother. *This letter must be a cruel joke*, she thought. He had to know this would hurt me. He is my twin.

Rose could not bear to look at Sarah, so, she busied herself at the sink washing her coffee cup. She knew her daughter was hurting but felt the hurt would go away with time.

"Mom."

"Yes, Sarah."

"I don't understand. He promised me when we started kindergarten, we would always be there for one another, remember?"

"No, Sarah, I don't remember that."

"Well, I do. On our first day of school, he said he would always be there for me, and I promised I would always be there for him. You and Daddy walked us to school. Before you left us, you asked if we knew our way back home. I told you I didn't have to know as long as my brother knew. Robert then said to you and Daddy, 'Sarah is right because I will always be there for my sister.' Don't you remember that?" Tears ran down Sarah's face. She sat trying to understand what she had just read. "Mom, what happened? Why did Robert leave? Did I do something? Is he angry with me?"

"What did he tell you in the note?"

"He said he wanted to see what was out there."

"Well, there you go. Robert is a man now. He has graduated from high school and wants to see what's waiting for him out in the world."

"What about college? I just don't understand why he had to leave without saying goodbye to me. Why did he have to do it in a note?" Tears continued streaming down Sarah's face. "I hate him! I hate him!" Sarah yelled as she started to leave the kitchen.

Rose turned around. "Stop right there, young lady. I don't want to hear that kind of talk from you. Your brother has gone out to make his own way in this world. Why are you so upset? You will be going off to college." Sarah stood with her back to her mother. "Turn around and look at me, young lady!"

Sarah turned, pouting, breathing hard, trying to hold back any audible sounds of anger, fear, pain, and sadness. Her feelings were a whirlwind of emotions settling in the pit of her stomach.

Looking at the sadness that covered her daughter's face and permeated down her body, Rose opened her mouth to say something to Sarah but decided against it. Instead, she said. "Sit back down and eat your breakfast."

Sarah sat back in her seat as her mother instructed. No longer hungry, she pushed the butter around on her cold pancakes. Sarah looked at the empty chair across the table in front of her, where Robert would have been sitting. Mouthwatering, she felt like she was about to vomit, so she swallowed hard. Then she asked to be excused.

Feeling uneasy, Rose got another cup from the cupboard and poured herself a second cup of coffee, after which she said, "Yes, you may be excused."

Sarah picked up the envelope which contained her brother's note. On her way to her room, she stopped at Robert's bedroom door and stared at it. After she entered her room, she slammed her door behind her. The noise startled Rose. She started to go to Sarah but changed her mind.

A part of who she was had walked out of the door with no departing words. After reading the note for the fifth time, Sarah sat in the middle of the bed and cried herself to sleep.

CHAPTER TWENTY-SEVEN

Rose and Sarah

Morsels of scripture weren't always enough for the conversations of the righteous. After Charlie's death, Rose and her children started attending church regularly. She even played for the senior choir on the third Sundays. Robert's decision to leave home the day after graduation gave the church saints a tasty bone to gnaw on. On Sunday mornings, the worship song should have been *I Love to Tell the Story*. The good Christians at church all had their versions of a story as to why Robert left home. They enjoyed partaking in the tasty morsels of gossip. Sarah saw the side glances people gave her mother. While smiling and grinning at one another, they huddled in small groups with their fans fluttering back and forth. When Rose walked by, the fans flittered faster than a hummingbird's wings. They avoided making eye contact with her, but as she walked past, their heads tilted in her direction like synchronized swimmers. They looked at her from the corner of their eyes and then gave each other an 'oh child' look while snickering behind her back. The rumor mill was that Robert had run away from home because he was ashamed of his colored mama.

It was nothing new for Rose. She knew what they were saying. On the Sundays when she played piano, she played with great fervor because the piano keys became the faces of the church gossipers. She knew her son hadn't run away from home. The gossipers would never dare say anything to her face because she had become the landlord for some of them after Charlie died.

* * *

Going away to college did nothing to fill the vacant space Robert left in her heart. Sarah spent many nights falling asleep in a fetal position in his bed. She wondered if he missed her as much as she missed him. Thoughts of her brother and her father covered her like a blanket. She remembered how she loved it when she and Robert heard their father's key in the door; they would run and hide. He would come in with a treat, and they would jump out from their hiding places and yell, "boo." Then he would grab his chest like he was surprised. Giggling and overcome with pure joy, they would jump on him and wrestle him to the living room floor. Rose would always come in right on cue and announce dinner. Sarah wished she could go back to that place in time.

Sarah had yet to hear from Robert on any birthdays or when she graduated from college. She didn't know if he was living or dead except for rumors. The two most influential men in her life were gone.

A Mother's White Lie

CHAPTER TWENTY-EIGHT

Sarah

Friday, June 18, 1976. It was thirty years to the day. Except for his room, it was like he never existed. Sarah and Rose started their day sitting on the side of their beds, thinking about Robert; his name never crossed their lips when they were together. But when alone, they both quietly whispered his name in the privacy of their bedrooms.

Sarah sat and waited to hear the stairs creak. Even though it was summer vacation, the morning routine was the same. Rose was up at 6:00 AM. Sarah heard the water running in the bathroom. Rose then dressed, went to the kitchen, made coffee, and cooked breakfast.

It was now her time to get into the bathroom. Looking in the medicine cabinet mirror, she saw Robert looking back at her.

After she dressed, she began descending the stairs. Upon reaching the fourth step, she hesitated and reversed her decision. Standing with her right foot on the fourth step and her left on the third, she turned to ascend back to Robert's room. She laid her hand against the closed door as though attempting to revive a still heart. Suddenly, a sharp knock at the front door jolted her. Inhaling deeply, she hurried down the stairs, yelling, "Mom, I've got it!"

Opening the door, Sarah saw him standing there, bronzed, like the sun had kissed his skin. His smile was so broad it showed every tooth in his mouth. "James!"

James had been accepted at Howard and he had hoped he and Robert would have attended Howard together, but after Robert's abrupt departure, James decided to attend Virginia Theological Seminary and College. That way, he would be close by for his aunt and his sister. He stayed in Lynchburg until his Aunt Rachael died in 1954. After Rachael's death, James moved to Richmond. Like Sarah, he had gone into education. He taught physical education and coached football. Even though he was only two hours away, he rarely visited. He frequently told himself he should do better, but he had been devastated by Robert's departure and Rachael's death.

Grabbing his arm, Sarah pulled him into the house. "Come in … come in!" Yelling while pulling him through the living room, "Mom, look who's here!"

Emerging from the kitchen and seeing James, Rose let out a shrilled giggle. She stood briefly with her hands over her mouth while tears rested on the edge of her lower eyelids. She raised outstretched arms, "Oh my goodness! James! What wind blew you in?"

He looked at his sister and trembled like a puppy, happy to see its owner. "I was feeling a little homesick. I missed everybody." He walked into his sister's open arms. He held her so tight and so close she could feel his heart beating.

A Mother's White Lie

Laughing, "Boy, I'm glad to see you, but I can't breathe."

He released his grip.

Adjusting her apron, she grabbed his arm, "Let me look at you. You look good. Come on into the kitchen. Are you hungry?" He followed Rose into the kitchen with Sarah walking on his heels. Not giving him a chance to answer, "Sit down. I was about to cook breakfast."

Pulling a chair out from the kitchen table, James looked at Sarah, "Here you go."

Shaking her head, "No, you sit there."

He responded, "Please let me be a gentleman." Sarah sat in the seat James had pulled out for her. "You know you're my decrepit aunt."

They both laughed. James had always joked with Robert and Sarah about them being only a few days older than him, their uncle. He smiled, almost laughing, remembering their childhood conversation. *Uncles are usually older than their nieces and nephews. Our folks got that all wrong. Your grandma and my sister were doing the hokey pokey around the same time.*

Witnessing his mischievous smile, Sarah said, "I know what you are smiling about, hokey pokey." They threw their heads back. Their boisterous laughter filled the kitchen and vibrated through the house.

It had been years since Rose and Charlie's special place had this kind of laughter. Rose's joy caused a twinge in the pit of her stomach. With her hands on her hips, she turned from the stove, "What's so funny?"

Giggling like two adolescents, Sarah and James responded in unison like members of a speech choir, "Nothing!"

A warm feeling washed over her as she stood watching James. He looked so much like their mother. Shaking her head, she returned to the stove and put a thick piece of country ham in a hot cast iron frying pan, causing grease to pop, as the ham sizzled, releasing a mouth-watering aroma.

Still laughing to herself, Sarah touched his forearm and said, "Please sit down. Would you like a cup of coffee?"

"Only if you're going to have a cup with me," James responded as he sat in a chair facing the open kitchen door with his back against the wall.

"I can do that." She pushed her chair from the table, reached over Rose's head, retrieved two cups from the cupboard, and placed them on the counter adjacent to the stove.

James rose from his seat and headed towards the open door, "Gosh! I remember this yard being so much larger."

Wiping her hands on a dishcloth, Rose walked over to him. Hugging him from behind, "Everything seems larger when you're a kid. I'm so glad you're here."

"I'm glad to be here." He took his seat at the table.

Sarah taking the aluminum percolator coffee pot from the stove, asked, "Would you like cream and sugar?"

"No, thank you."

Sarah filled the cups with steaming black coffee. Careful not to spill a drop, she sauntered across the kitchen and placed the two cups on the table: one in front of James and the other in front of the chair where she was sitting. Rose busied herself, pulling out cast iron skillets. Soon the aroma of fried country ham mingled with fried potatoes with onions, hot buttered biscuits, and apple butter.

Sipping his coffee, James smiled. "This smells like home."

Glancing at James over her shoulder, she smiled. Rose hummed while she cooked. There was a joy in the air she hadn't felt in a long while. With James sitting there, it felt like she had a bit of her mother and her son with her, making her happy.

Cradling his cup in both hands, James blew on his coffee to cool it. Peering through the steam at Sarah, he said, "I have missed you all. How have you been?"

Sarah smiled. "I'm alright. We're alright."

Rose looked over her shoulder and smiled, "James, I'm great!"

Sarah shook her head and said, "Mom doesn't let anything bother her. Every day is pretty much the same."

Rose set two plates on the table, each piled high with country ham, scrambled eggs, fried potatoes with onions, and hot biscuits. She placed one in front of James and the other in front of Sarah.

James asked, "Where is your plate?"

"I just want coffee. Oh, here is some apple butter for your biscuits."

"You make me feel bad. You cooked all of this because of me?"

Sarah kicked James under the table, "James, don't argue with her. She cooks and fills my plate until it's running over with food. Then she sits and watches me eat."

James laughed, "Come sit and talk with me while we eat."

Rose poured herself a cup of coffee and sat at the table. "Tell me, baby brother, what brought you back home?"

"I was missing home." When James left home, he was running away from an emptiness he had felt ever since the day he understood his mother died after giving birth to him. He had never known what a mother's love felt like. His father was stern and unwavering. He had never shared with anyone that he felt his father and his siblings blamed him for their mother's death. The affection from his Aunt Rachael and his sister, Rose, was as close to what he imagined love from a mother would be like. He looked forward to the times Rachael would bring him to Lynchburg under the guise of going shopping, so he could spend time with Rose, Charlie, his niece, and nephew. Even though Charlie was white, James felt a caring from Charlie his father seemed incapable of giving. Running away did nothing to fill his emptiness because he carried his emptiness with him, so he decided it was time to stop running. It was time to come home.

Rose laughed, "It took you this long to miss home?"

"No." Looking around the kitchen, James took a deep breath. "Rose, can I ask you something?"

"Of course. What is it?"

His throat felt like he had a lump of coal in it, making it difficult to speak. He coughed to clear it. "Did you blame me for our mother's death?"

Frowning, "No! Why would you think something like that?"

"Daddy…."

"James, Daddy didn't always know how to show love. The man you saw and lived with was the same man I lived with. It had nothing to do with you being born or Mama dying."

As Sarah and James ate, the room was filled with silence, broken only by the sound of clicking knives and forks. For James, the silence was unsettling. He could feel Rose's gaze on him, and he felt the urge to break the silence. So, just as James was about to put a fork of scrambled eggs into his mouth, he stopped the fork in mid-air and said, "The neighborhood has changed a lot. That old wooden hotel on the corner of Fifth and Polk is gone, and there is a new brick building there."

Lynchburg's Fifth Street had undergone many changes. Before it became a hub for Black businesses, it had several names: Seventh Alley, Cocke Street, and West Street. It was also the highway that connected Maryland to Florida.

"Yes, the brick building is the Johnson Building. That old hotel was about to collapse, but it was listed in the Green Book. The neighborhood has changed. Fifth Street was once a mecca of Negro businesses. There were doctors, lawyers, a bakery, Johnnie Franklin's Wood and Coal Shack, restaurants, Reid's Pharmacy, Harrison Movie Theater, hairdressers, barber shops, funeral homes, Leon Gibson's Watch Repair Shop, and Miller's Grocery Store – all on Fifth Street. We had what we needed right here. We only had to leave the community to work and to go to the hospital."

James put his fork on his plate and sat back in his chair. "Wow! But what was the Green Book?"

"It was a little green book with a list of safe places where we, Black people, could eat and stay when traveling," Rose explained. Her voice softened. "Charlie and I never traveled anywhere. I don't want to imagine what would have happened if we had been caught traveling together." Rose got up to freshen her coffee.

The room was once again filled with sadness. Sarah and James exchanged glances. Suddenly, Sarah blurted out, "Do you remember Mamie Feimster?"

Pouring coffee into her cup, Rose gazed across the room at Sarah and inquired, "Where did that come from?"

Hunching her shoulders, Sarah said, "I don't know."

James responded, "I think I remember that story. Wasn't she shot by one of her girls?"

Sarah answered, "Yes, but I don't remember the name of the girl who shot her, but didn't she shoot one of the other girls too?"

Rose stood at the sink with her back to them, saying, "Buckwalter."

Puzzled, Sarah asked, "Mom?"

Rose turned to face them, "Her name was Buckwalter … Lythia Buckwalter."

"Yeah, that was her name. Mom, you have a memory like an elephant," Sarah responded.

Rose chuckled, "That was the talk of the neighborhood. This little white woman shooting two other white women. I remember the newspaper story said Buckwalter met the police at the door with a Smith & Wesson in her hand, and Mamie was lying in a pool of blood on the kitchen floor and there was a bowl of chicken broth cooling on the kitchen table."

James chuckled, "That's crazy!"

Rose responded, "No, crazy is a judge sending his bailiff to Fourth Street to retrieve his pocket watch he had left the night before."

Shocked but amused, James asked. "What? Wasn't what they were doing against the law?"

Sarah mumbled, "Who makes the laws?"

Rose looked from Sarah to James and said, "Yes, but the rumor was one morning when Judge McCarron came to work, he realized he had left his pocket watch on the dresser at Tootsie's place. So, he sent his bailiff to get it."

Laughing, James said, "Wow!"

"A lot of crazy things happened in that redlight district on Fourth Street." Rose returned to her seat at the table. "I thought we were talking about the Black businesses."

James laughed, "We just got a little sidetracked."

Sarah looked up from her plate. "A lot of our Black businesses are gone now, but I remember some of those businesses that were on Fifth Street. Integration changed a lot of things. Once we no longer had to ride on the back of the bus, and we could eat at what had been white-only counters, we stopped supporting businesses in our neighborhood."

"Integration did kill our businesses." Staring into her coffee cup, in a low soft voice, Rose said, "If Charlie and I had met during this time, he might still be alive."

Sarah and James exchanged glances again. It seemed impossible to discuss the past without sadness filling the room. "Mom, what do you mean by Dad might still be alive?"

With a sad smile, Rose responded, "I didn't mean anything. What I'm saying is we could be married."

Looking out the kitchen door, James said, "I remember Aunt Rachael telling me how you and Charlie exchanged your own vows under that pear tree out there."

Rose sighed, "Yes, that pear tree is special."

"Mom, do you think you would've been accepted in a white neighborhood the way Dad was accepted here?"

Feeling a bit irritated by her daughter's question, "No! I wouldn't have been. I would've been jailed or killed. Besides, this was Charlie's house. He owned it! It was no one's business but ours: he lived here with me."

James lowered his eyes. Sarah reached over and placed her hand over the top of her mother's clinched hands resting on the table. She could feel her mother trembling. "Mom, I didn't mean to upset you."

Rose responded, lying, "I'm not upset."

As children, Sarah, Robert, and James were aware that the relationship between Rose and Charlie was considered taboo. They knew that their two worlds were different. What was accepted in one world was blatantly not accepted in the other. Now, Sarah wonders if the law enforcement officials in Lynchburg turned a blind eye to her parents' cohabitation because they were involved in unlawful activities just around the corner from her parents' residence.

Trying to alleviate the tension in the air, Rose said, "James, you haven't eaten very much."

James chuckled, "I'm taking my time. I want to savor every bite. I don't know when I will have another meal like this."

Rose reached over to touch her brother's hand. "How long are you going to be here?"

"I haven't decided."

"Where are you staying?"

"I haven't decided that either."

Rose patted his hand again. "You will stay here. You don't mind sleeping on the sofa, do you?"

CHAPTER TWENTY-NINE

Sarah and James

James and Sarah sat in rocking chairs on the front porch drinking sweet tea with mint and lemon while Rose busied herself preparing a feast for the last day of James's visit. Not a single cloud dotted the sky. The scent of roses wafted on a warm breeze from a rose bush in the yard, which Sarah and Robert had planted in memory of their father. It appeared oddly placed, but the rose bush and the place in the street where their father had been killed were in close juxtaposition. Miss Minor was sweeping her porch; a couple of neighbors waved as they walked by, and Sarah and James smiled and waved back. Miss Bessie stood with her body partly on the porch and partly behind the front door. Two little boys raced up Fourth Street, one yelling, "Let's cut through the cemetery." There was a railroad track behind the cemetery. James and Robert would cut through the cemetery as kids and followed the railroad track to Blackwater Creek to go fishing.

Sarah laughed jovially. "I remember the days!"

"What are you laughing about?"

"Do you remember the story of the Green-Eyed Monster who lived in the cemetery?"

James chuckled. "I sure do. I think the keepers of the cemetery started that story to keep us from cutting through the cemetery. But it didn't work."

"Oh, but it did work."

"No, not really, because we cut through the cemetery whenever Robert and I went fishing."

"That was during daylight. I think the Green-Eyed Monster was created to keep lovers out of the cemetery at night."

They chuckled, then a hush fell over as they observed cars passing by, children frolicking, and neighbors tending to their yards.

Inhaling deeply, "The air around this house always smelled so sweet during the summer."

"Yeah, from the Sweet Peas and Snap Dragons Daddy planted and the rose bush we planted."

James looked over at Sarah. For five days, he honored what seemed to be an unspoken vow between Sarah and Rose. Neither allowed Robert's name to pass through their lips, but he had not made that vow. "Sarah, why don't you or Rose talk about him?"

Pretending not to know of whom he was speaking, Sarah responded, "Who? Talk about who?"

"Come on, Sarah, Robert. I have been here six days, and it's like he never existed."

"James, I've tried talking about him. Every time I try, Mom changes the subject, or she walks out of the room, but I know she is always expecting to hear from him."

"Why do you say that?"

"Haven't you noticed she meets the mailman every day? I'm not allowed to get the mail."

"What? I haven't noticed."

"Two days after Robert left, Mom started waiting for the mailman at the front door or on the porch. If I attempted to get the mail, she would tell me she would get it. She sorts through the mail, and she gives me my mail. I don't talk about him, and I don't get the mail."

"Do you think she has heard from him or has any idea where he is?"

"No, I don't think so. I feel if she knew where he is she would talk about him. I've heard rumors about him being in New York. I've also heard rumors about him crossing the color line, but I don't want to believe he would do that. Do you?"

"I've heard the same rumors you've heard. To be honest, I don't know what to think. What does Rose think?"

Rose opened the screen door and stepped onto the porch. James stood up, offering Rose his seat. Facing Sarah and Rose, he leaned on the green railing that ran the length of the porch, supported by spindles. "Do I smell an apple pie cooking?"

Rose laughed, "No, baby brother. It's an apple cobbler."

Laughing and rubbing his stomach, "Oh, that's even better. You got any vanilla ice cream to go on top?"

Giving a hearty laugh, "I sure do! I also made some potato salad, macaroni and cheese, corn pudding, country ham, green beans, and I'm gonna fry up some chicken."

James held up his hand for Rose to halt. "Rose don't fry chicken. You have cooked enough."

Sarah leaned forward, playfully slapped James's leg, and said, "Don't waste your breath, James. She's going to fry chicken."

"Never mind what I'm cooking. What have the two of you been talking about?"

Sarah was about to respond with "nothing," but James spoke before she could part her lips. "I was just asking Sarah about Robert."

Sarah pushed herself back into her chair. She braced herself for a storm. James had crossed over into a forbidden topic of conversation.

A scowl crawled across Rose's face like a storm cloud slowly covering the sun. She leaned forward and peered down the street. Then Rose turned to Sarah, "Have you seen the mailman? He's running a little late today."

Sarah and James's eyes met. Sarah shrugged, responding, "I haven't seen him." Sarah knew this was her mother's way of deflecting the conversation. She had been annoyed in the past when her mother did this. At this moment, she had an appreciative attitude because she wasn't about to partake in the conversation James was hellbent on having. So, she repositioned herself in the rocker, with her back slightly turned away from Rose and James. She focused on several little girls playing hopscotch in the street.

James wasn't about to be ignored. "Rose, don't you miss Robert? Don't you want to know where he is?"

Tapping her left foot on the concrete porch, she sat silently for a moment. She didn't want to be rude to her brother, but what he was asking wasn't his concern. She took a deep breath and slowly let it out. Then she responded, "He is my child! Of course, I miss him."

Continuing to probe for answers, James asked, "Have you considered hiring someone to find him?"

Rose spoke slowly and deliberately. "No, I haven't. I don't feel he needs to be found."

Upon hearing her mother's tone and words, Sarah's brow furrowed. She could sense her mother's anger and hearing her say that she didn't feel Robert needed to be found hurt Sarah deeply. She fought back tears as her mind raced. *Why would her mother say this? Did she and Robert have a disagreement? Was that the reason he left? What does her mother know that she hasn't shared?*

Sarah's barrage of mental questions stopped when she felt angry heat radiating from her mother. She steadied herself and waited for the volcano to erupt.

Rose rocked her chair forward and stood up. She was now standing face to face with James; she gave him a sarcastic smile, "James, this is really none of your business." She took a moment to compose herself. "Besides, in my heart, I feel Robert is alright, and he'll come home when he's ready."

Grabbing Rose's hand, James started to speak, "I will…."

Looking directly into his eyes, she snatched her hand away; Rose interrupted him declaring, "I have nothing else to say, James." She walked to the edge of the porch.

James moved from the railing back to the chair he had given Rose, he took a breath to speak, but Sarah put her finger to her lips to hush him. Heeding her gesture, he sat quietly, looking at his sister's back. Nothing was said. Rose stepped off the porch and walked to the front gate. She watched the girls hopping on one leg from one square to another they had drawn in the street. The silence was finally broken when Rose gleefully said, "Here comes the mailman."

James and Sarah leaned forward in their seats to peer down the sidewalk. The mailman, a tall, slender man with salt and pepper hair, approached Rose.

"Hi, Miss Rose. How are you today?"

"I'm fine. Do you have anything for me today?"

Handing her the mail he had in his hands, "Miss Rose, it smells like you're cooking something good today."

Reaching for the mail he was handing her, she laughed. "Yes, I have a cobbler in the oven. Just cooking up a little something for my baby brother here."

The mailman peeped over at Sarah and James and tilted his hat. "Smells like y'all will be eating good today. Miss Rose, I'll see you tomorrow. Y'all have a good day now."

Rose smiled and said, "Okay. You have a good day too." Rose sorted through the mail. She handed Sarah all the mail except one envelope.

Not wanting to give James more opportunity to ask about Robert, Rose opened the screen door and stepped into the house. She walked hurriedly into the kitchen and put the envelope on the table. She took a glass from the cupboard and filled it with water from the spigot. She placed the glass on the table, pulled the chair out, and lowered her body into it. Then she planted her feet on the floor and scooted her chair under the table. With closed eyes, she picked up the envelope and held it to her chest. It was from Robert.

A Mother's White Lie

CHAPTER THIRTY

James

December 18, 1976, James wasn't seeking the truth, but the truth stumbled into him. He arrived in Baltimore the day before the Baltimore Colts and Pittsburgh Steelers game. It was a pre-Christmas gift to himself. After checking into his hotel, James's growling stomach demanded food. He stepped out into the frigid evening air, feeling the cold, damp wind blowing in from Baltimore Harbor. The moon was peeking from behind clouds, and he had a taste for Italian food. Since his car was parked and he didn't want to venture into the section of Baltimore known as Little Italy, he decided to find somewhere to dine within walking distance of his hotel. Pulling up his coat collar to cover his ears, he shoved his hands into his coat pockets, took a deep breath, and started his hunt for food. He turned onto Eutaw Street and noticed The Palmer House. Although he had heard of the place, he had never dined there before. Because he didn't have a reservation, he had a thirty-minute wait. That wasn't a problem. It was warm. Looking around, he saw pictures of celebrities, Joe Louis, Babe Ruth, Herbert Hoover, Bob Hope, Elvis, and many others, covering the walls.

While he waited, the maître d' asked if he would be interested in having his fortune told. *That'll be entertaining*, James thought. Smiling, he gave an affirmative nod. The maître d' directed him to a table in the waiting area.

There was a dowdy middle-aged woman with red hair sitting at the table. Heavy makeup sat between the crevices of wrinkles on her face. She smiled widely, exposing all her teeth, and with a wave of her hand, directed James to sit in the chair directly across from her. While shuffling a deck of cards, she asked him if he had ever had his fortune told before. He hadn't. She handed him the deck of cards and directed him to shuffle and cut them with his left hand. James chuckled and after shuffling the cards, he placed them on the table and cut them with his left hand. Laughing, he asked, "Why the left hand?"

She didn't answer him but smiled and said, "Please follow me closely. You don't have to confirm or deny anything unless you wish to do so. Please select one of the piles of cards."

James pointed to one of the two piles of cards sitting on the table. She instructed him to pick up the pile and hand it to her. He did as she instructed. She counted seventeen cards and placed them on the table in several rows. She looked at the cards. She pointed to the queen of clubs and the three of hearts and said, "I see a dark woman who is a true friend to you. The three of hearts tells me she is very kind. I can't tell if she is a mother or maybe a mother figure."

James smiled. He was having a conversation in his head. He didn't believe in fortune tellers but was impressed with what she said. *She must be talking about my Aunt Rachael. No, she said the woman is a friend, so it must be my sister Rose.*

Holding the king of diamonds, "I see a man who will be coming back into your life. It appears he has been living with a secret. I see the mother figure I spoke of is somehow connected to this man. He is a caring man. He seems to be carrying a heavy burden."

James's face became serious. A frown slowly crawled across his brow.

Her eyes met James's gaze. "Are you alright?"

Laughing sheepishly, he responded, "Yes." But he wasn't okay. He was troubled by what she had said. Beads of sweat erupted from his face like kernels in a popper. He took out a handkerchief from his jacket to wipe his face.

She waved her hand over the ace of spades. She looked up at him. Their eyes again locked in a stare.

When she opened her mouth to speak, the maître d' interrupted. "I can seat you now."

He tucked the handkerchief back into his pocket and felt relief. He looked at the maître d' and said, "Thank you!" Then, turning to the woman who was staring at the ace of spades, he said, "Thank you. I think I've heard enough." The woman nodded. He pushed his chair back and followed the maître d' to a small table covered with a white tablecloth.

After consuming several glasses of chianti, a hearty serving of spaghetti with marinara sauce, and garlic bread, James's hunger was satiated. However, his mind remained in a state of confusion. He donned his coat and pulled up the collar. Stepping outside the restaurant, a frigid wind slapped him across his face. His breath formed a cloud that hung motionless in the air, akin to the words of the dowdy red-headed woman still lingering in his mind.

A Mother's White Lie

CHAPTER THIRTY-ONE

James

December 19, 1976. The last evening at the Palmer House was interesting and occupied James's thoughts until he fell asleep. But today was a new day. He looked forward to sitting in Memorial Stadium, eating a Polock Johnny's hotdog, drinking beer, and cheering as the Baltimore Colts trampled the Pittsburgh Steelers. He ate his hotdog, drank his beer, and cheered for the Colts, but the Steelers trampled the Colts 40-14. An unwavering Colts enthusiast, James stayed until the end of the game. He was on his way out of the stadium when a commotion ensued. The sound of a loud noise prompted people to start running, and amidst the chaos, he heard a voice shouting about a plane crashing near section one of the stadium. Dazed by the realization he had just left the very area where the plane had crashed, he stood still amongst a sea of people pushing past him to the exit. In the crowd, going toward the locker room, James thought he saw a familiar face. He tried to see above the crowd but was pushed in a swelling wave of people towards the exit. Once outside, he mumbled a prayer of thanks.

He always looked forward to visiting Lenny Moore's Sportsman's Club in Baltimore to listen to some great jazz. Tonight, he needed it more than ever. As he stepped into the club, the music surrounded him. He walked through a haze of lingering cigarette smoke. The club was packed, but he managed to find a seat at the end of the bar, facing the main entrance. The band was playing Miles Davis's *Whispering*. The bartender, a man in his mid-thirties, strolled to the end of the bar. "Good evening, man. It's a great day to be alive. What will you have this evening?"

James choked back laughter, "You're so right! Give me two fingers of bourbon."

"You got it!" Wiping his hands on a towel stuck in his belt, the bartender placed a glass on the bar in front of James. He poured two fingers of Jim Beam. "Enjoy."

As James inhaled the aroma of his drink, he took a gulp. feeling a burning sensation in his throat and a subsequent warmth spreading through his chest, leading to a sense of relaxation in his body. James leaned against the wall and observed women entering the club. A young woman with cocoa-colored skin, dressed in a white pantsuit and a white coordinating head wrap, caught his attention. His eyes followed her as she and her friends found seats at a table situated near the band. The waiter went over to take their drink order. James signaled the bartender when he came to the bar with the order. He requested that the bartender send the young lady in white two of whatever she ordered. When the waiter delivered the drinks, he pointed to James. She leaned over to see. James smiled, and she smiled back. After five minutes of talking and giggling with her girlfriends, she made her way to the end of the bar to express gratitude to James. Before she could say anything, James greeted her with, "So what."

With her hands on her hips and a slight head tilt, she retorted, "I beg your pardon."

He laughed, "The band is playing *So What* by Miles Davis.

She laughed and asked, "So what ... are you expecting for the drinks you sent me?"

He smiled and said, "Nothing. What would make you think I'd want something other than your name?" He knowingly misrepresented himself as he was primarily focused on achieving physical intimacy rather than establishing genuine rapport. After forty-five minutes and three Singapore Slings, he ascertained that her name was Roberta. She disclosed that she worked as a reading instructor for junior high school students and was currently enjoying the Christmas break. Subsequently, he initiated physical contact by taking her hand and leading her in a swaying motion in rhythm to the music. Putting his tongue in her ear, he whispered, "Do you want to get out of here?" Just as the words tumbled from his mouth, he glimpsed the familiar face he thought he had spotted earlier heading toward the stadium's locker rooms.

Feeling lightheaded and giddy, Roberta queried about the whereabouts of their destination while playfully sticking her tongue in James's ear. The hair stood up on the back of his neck. James stood silently for a moment. He gently moved her aside, asking her for a rain check. He walked past her and over to a man standing by the door, "Robert?" The two men stood staring at one another.

A Mother's White Lie

CHAPTER THIRTY-TWO

Robert

Had he created his identity, or had it just happened? Robert questioned whether he created his own identity or if it evolved organically since his departure from home in June 1949. He convinced himself that it simply occurred. He directed his life's course, and events unfolded. Despite living in fear, he pursued a life devoid of it. This life afforded him the freedom to pursue his desires, travel where he pleased, and reside in his chosen location. It also granted him the privilege of riding at the front of the bus. His life and perception of reality were influenced by how others perceived him. That was Robert's question since he left home in June of 1949.

After the game, he only wanted to relax with a few drinks and listen to music. He was in Baltimore on an assignment to cover the Pittsburgh vs. Colts game. He should've known his love for music would one day put him in a place where he would collide with his past. He had played the scenario over in his mind a thousand times, but it had always been with someone he knew from home, not a family member.

Robert examined his reflection in the full-length mirror of James's hotel lobby. He flicked away a speck of lint from the black velvet collar of his Chesterfield coat. His appearance was slightly haggard, as sleep had eluded him the night before. The prospect of reuniting with his uncle filled him with excitement, yet the idea of answering questions or recounting the past twenty-seven years filled him with dread. Upon entering the bar, he noticed James already seated in a booth by the entrance, sipping on a bourbon. Robert observed that James was the sole patron in the bar, which wasn't unusual since most people attended church at eleven on a Sunday morning. With no possibility of retreat, Robert's approach to the booth, where James awaited, felt akin to marching toward his own execution.

James gave a cursory glance at him before Robert took off his coat and neatly folded it in half. He draped it over his arm before he placed it on the seat and pushed it to the corner of the booth before he sat down. James sat silently, watching Robert positioning himself in the booth. Stirring his drink with his finger, James looked across the booth at Robert. "Look at you, man. I guess the rumors I heard are true."

Looking at James directly, Robert responded with, "What rumors?"

Squinting his eyes, James spoke, "The rumor of you leaving home to live as a white man."

Clasping his hands on the table, Robert asked, "Isn't that what we all do in life?"

Shaking his head, James didn't say anything for a moment, then he asked himself, *who is this person?* This wasn't the uncle he had grown up with. With raised brows, James took a large sip of his drink and asked, "What do you mean by that?"

Clearing his throat, Robert asked, "Wasn't it Shakespeare who said, *All the world's a stage, and all the men and women merely players; they have their exits and their entrances; and one man in his time plays many parts*?"

James was becoming agitated by Robert's pestilent attitude. He had to stop himself from reaching across the table to strike Robert. "Shakespeare! What the hell are you talking about? You hurt people, and you're sitting here trivializing what you did."

"No, I'm not! Don't we all live our lives acting? Acting like we are happy when we're sad. Acting like we care when we really don't. Acting like we're single when we are really married. Acting the way people think we should. Acting like we are...."

An emaciated-looking blond waitress with ruby red lipstick interrupted Robert, "Hello. What can I get for you?"

Slightly nodding towards James, Robert replied, "I'll take what he has. And bring him another."

"You got it!" As she walked away, Robert noticed she walked with a limp. Her left leg appeared to be shorter than her right leg. He wondered about her story. He turned back to meet a stare from James. Robert saw puzzlement all over his uncle's face. He knew he had to provide James with some answers. They sat for a moment in awkward silence.

James shook his head in disdain and broke the silence with a disheartened sigh. "You have the nerve to sit here talking about acting. If you are going to bring Shakespeare into this, do you recall what a tangled web we weave when we try to deceive? Man, I don't get you! I don't understand how you could just walk away like that. Don't you have feelings? You just turned your back on your mother and your sister. What was going through your mind? Are they too black for you? I'm begging you for an explanation."

Robert lowered his head. Not knowing whether to feel angry or insulted, he could feel his face turning red and the knuckles of his tightly clasped hands were white. He knew he had to share his truth. Flattening his hands on the table, words started tumbling from his lips. "First, let me say I didn't just walk away." After the first words left his mouth, he felt a lightness he hadn't felt since he left home. "Leaving home wasn't my idea. It was Mom's. I…."

James felt intense anger when Robert laid the responsibility for his actions on his sister. "What are you saying? Are you saying it was Rose's idea for you to leave home and pass for white?"

Robert never realized the truth would be so liberating. "That's exactly what I'm saying. I have written to Mom at least twice a month for the last twenty-seven years. I had hoped Sarah would see my letters, but Mom told me she's always there when the mailman comes."

James didn't want to believe what he was hearing, but he remembered when he was visiting Rose and Sarah, Rose came out to meet the mailman. He remembered she sorted through it before giving Sarah her mail. A shadow of disapproval crept across his face. Even though his mind believed what he was hearing, his heart had a hard time accepting the possibility his sister had anything to do with Robert's decision to pass for white. "Even if Rose told you to do this, you didn't have to. And why didn't you write Sarah?"

"I know…." His words halted abruptly as he noticed the waitress, limping with a tray of drinks in hand, approaching their table. It was then he realized that he and James weren't the only patrons in the bar anymore. An elderly couple had taken seats at the bar, their expressions etched with sorrow. Perhaps they were attempting to drown their melancholy in alcohol. They seemed like regulars, given the bartender's familiar interaction with the woman, even reaching out to clasp her hand in an apparent gesture of comfort.

The waitress placed the drinks on the table in front of Robert. "Can I get you anything else?"

Robert replied, "No, thank you."

As she limped away, James said, "Wow!"

"What?"

"You didn't notice, did you?"

"Notice what?"

"That I became invisible the moment you sat down here. She placed both drinks in front of you. And she asked if she could get you anything else. She never looked at me. Didn't you notice, she positioned herself, so her back was turned slightly to me? And you didn't notice. Wow!" James took another large gulp of his drink.

Robert was uneasy, feeling a pang of shame for his obliviousness. His visibility had always been a given; in his neighborhood, it was his skin color that made him stand out, and in the white world, he blended in seamlessly. He understood that no words could ease the hurt that James was enduring. The waitress's behavior only intensified the existing discomfort.

James could see that Robert was feeling uneasy. He took a certain pleasure in observing him, at a loss for words. Watching his uncle dodge his gaze and fidget with his drink, James asked, "Why didn't you contact Sarah? She's not just your sister; she is your twin!"

Robert looked up from his drink, "Mom asked me not to. I hoped she would see one of the letters I wrote Mom."

"Man, I just don't understand. Tell me what Rose said when she told you to pass for white." He took another gulp from his drink. "What exactly did she say to you?"

"James, Mom did what she did out of love."

"Man, she had two children. Are you telling me she doesn't love Sarah?"

"She loves Sarah. Let me just tell you how I think it all started. You remember I had that after-school job downtown cleaning offices?"

"Yeah, I remember. We both did."

"Well, one day, I was too tired to walk home, so I caught the bus. When I got on the bus that day, there were no seats available. The bus driver got up and made an elderly Black man get up so I could sit. I was shocked."

Frowning and slightly tilting his head, James asked, "You took the seat?"

"Yes. I was scared. I was afraid to tell the bus driver the truth." Running his finger around the rim of his glass, he continued his story. "When I got home, I told Mom what happened. She looked at me and nodded. Then she told me the best thing she could do for me after I graduated from school was to have me leave home. To go to New York and pass for white. I didn't think she meant it. I thought she was joking, but right before graduation, she repeated it."

"So, you live in New York?"

"Yes. I asked her, 'What about Sarah?' Mom said she wanted us both to have the best that life could offer us. She told me she would make sure Sarah completed college. She said she would send me money for school. When I got to New York, I found a job and paid my way through college, taking night classes."

"I can't believe this."

"Mom said it would be best if I cut off all contact with family. She thought it would protect me from people finding out, but I couldn't break contact with her. Now, before I say anything else to you, I'm asking you to keep this to yourself. You haven't seen or spoken to me. I'll come home on my own time. When I decide the time, I want to be the one to tell Sarah why I left. Promise me."

A Mother's White Lie

James sat silently, looking at Robert. He took a sip of his drink. He looked around the bar. Several other people had come in. "I don't know if I can promise that. You didn't see Sarah after you left. She grieved for you."

"I know because I grieved for her. I created this situation. It's my situation to clear up when I'm ready."

"You're right. You created this situation, so you should be the one to clean it up." Taking another sip of his drink, James said, "Robert, tell me about you. You said you're living in New York. What's it like being white? Are you happy?"

"Am I happy? I'm a journalist. I work for a prominent New York newspaper. I dine at some of the finest restaurants. I worked my way from the mailroom to becoming a reporter. I took journalism classes at night. I got my degree. Guess what my first big story was?"

James mumbled, "I don't know." He didn't care.

"The Emmett Till trial in Sumner, Mississippi."

James replied sarcastically, "How appropriate that your first big story was the murder of a Black boy."

Robert ignored James's snide remark. "When my boss called me into his office and told me he was sending me to Mississippi to cover the Emmett Till murder trial, I was excited. When I stepped into that courtroom, fear washed over me. I don't know what I expected. The room was small, sweltering hot, and packed to capacity. Some white male spectators wore guns. A few Black spectators stood in the back of the courtroom. Black and white reporters were not allowed to sit together. White reporters were seated behind the all-white male jurors in the jury box. I was shocked watching jurors drinking beer during the trial. It was a party for them. The sheriff had Black reporters, Medgar Evers, and Mamie Till at a card table by a window across the courtroom away from the jury. We were instructed, by the judge, not to take photographs during the proceedings." Robert noticed that the waitress was limping her way back towards the table. Robert held his hand up and shook his head to indicate she wasn't needed. Robert took a sip from his drink. "During the days of the trial, I met some of the Black reporters. They were good people."

James chuckled and repeated Robert's words, "They were good people."

It was hard for Robert not to hear the indignation in James's voice. "I felt ashamed of who I was, so, whenever I walked past the card table where the sheriff had put them...I mean the Black reporters ... the other reporters." Robert knew now he could say nothing right, but he continued talking. "I held my head down. If I looked at them, I feared they would know I was one of them ... I was Black. Those reporters had a courage I don't know if I will ever be capable of having. During the testimony of Moses Wright, I was sitting in the first chair behind the jurors. The table with the Black reporters was in my direct view. Moses was in the witness box, right next to the jury seats. When District Attorney Gerald Chatham asked Moses to point out Milam, the man who had come to his house and taken Emmett, a hush fell over that courtroom. When Moses rose from his seat in the witness box, I saw Ernest Withers, a Black reporter, position his camera on the table in Moses's direction. When Moses pointed at Milam, I saw Withers snap his camera. I was scared for him, but he wasn't caught. I have often wondered what made him take that picture. Moses and Withers both defied...."

Frustrated, James interrupted, "Why are you telling me all this?"

Robert sat staring at his hands on the table. Reliving this experience caused him to tremble. Clasping his hands together, he looked at James and responded, "Please be patient. I am trying to explain." He closed his eyes for a moment. When he opened them, he looked directly into James's eyes and said, "They were courageous. I wish I'd had the courage...." Robert hesitated again before continuing. "One morning, I was walking behind the sheriff. Strider. That was his name. I will never forget him. I was behind him as he walked past the table of Black reporters; he stopped, smiled, and said, 'Hello niggers.' He turned to face me and said, 'Wasn't it just like a nigger to try and cross the Tallahatchie River with a gin fan around his neck?' I felt sick. I listened to Carolyn Bryant, a mother of two boys, testify Emmett came into that store, grabbed her wrist and waist, and made lewd comments to her. Her words caused Emmett's death. I also listened as the prosecutors tried to discredit Emmett's mother. I couldn't imagine her pain as she sat there listening to testimony after testimony about her son. I thought about my mother. I realized then her way of protecting me from being an Emmett Till was to insist I cross the color line." Robert stopped talking to sip his drink. "In the evenings, I would return to my hotel room and cry. On the last day of the trial, I knew everyone knew Milam and Bryant were guilty, but it didn't matter. They all told their white lies, and Milam and Bryant were found not guilty. They celebrated with their children in the courtroom. They walked out free men. I was sick. After calling the story to my editor, I went to my hotel room and cried like a baby."

James felt no compassion. He looked at Robert with contempt in his eyes. He mumbled, "Words ... lies kill. You killed the uncle I knew with the lie you're living."

Robert lowered his head, then looked up and said, "You're right. Lies can kill. But they can protect! They can also keep you safe. When I saw Milam and Bryant walk out of that courthouse, I understood why my mom, your sister, wanted me to live this lie. It was her way of protecting her only son. It was her way of keeping me safe."

James allowed the words to hang in the air: "*It was her way of protecting her only son. It was her way of keeping me safe.*" He let them settle into his mind's recesses. James understood, although he wished he didn't. Anger began to stir within him, its source uncertain. Was it the fact that Robert was living a lie? Was it the idea that his sister had proposed such a deception? Or the notion that his sister believed a lie was the only refuge for her son? "Damn!" James drained his glass. He slammed the glass on the table and sat staring at his hand wrapped tightly around the empty glass.

Robert coughed to clear his throat. "I think I can use another drink."

James looked up at him.

"You asked me if I'm happy." Robert chuckled as though he was amused. "Happiness is relative. I live in fear. In fear of being found out." Even though he understood his mother thought a lie would protect him, he never realized the weight of that lie on his soul until this moment. Telling his truth, he felt lighter.

CHAPTER THIRTY-THREE

James

December 24, 1976. Promises are not made to be broken. James felt like the winter day – grey sky with low-hanging clouds. Being in Lynchburg for Christmas was not high on his agenda, but he had made a promise to Rose and Sarah. Regardless of how he felt, he loved the neighborhood. Children were laughing and playing – anticipating a visit from jolly old Saint Nicholas. Christmas trees with colored lights could be seen in the windows. James sniffed – the smells of Christmas were in the air. He could smell freshly baked yeast rolls, baked ham, chitterlings, apple pie, or cobbler—he didn't know which. He stood at the gate to Rose's house, remembering the smells of Christmas from his childhood: Creasy greens, cake, and roasting ham and turkey with stuffing intermingled with the smell of paste wax. Rachael would be busy cooking, while James took on the task of waxing the hardwood floors in the hallway. He chuckled heartily as he recalled polishing the floor by sliding on it with his backside. Rachael handed him a few old wool sweaters, and James would twist and turn on them, gliding up and down the hallway. Despite ending up with a couple of splinters, the floor gleamed as if it were brand new. He unlatched the gate, and as he stepped onto the porch, Sarah swung the door open.

Startled, James dropped the shopping bag he had containing gifts, "Were you standing waiting for me to knock?"

Sarah laughed, "No, but please come in. I was looking for Mom." Sarah stepped aside for James to enter.

He reached down to pick up the bag, "I am glad I had nothing breakable." He stepped into the house and handed the bag to Sarah, "Here are a couple of gifts to put under the tree."

Sarah laughed, "Can I get a hug first?"

He smiled and responded, "Of course." He put his arms around Sarah, giving her a halfhearted embrace, "Where is Rose?"

Sarah took two wrapped gifts from the bag and placed them under the tree. "Mom didn't say where she was going, but I would guess she is in Rustburg. She goes to Grandma's and Grandpa's graves every holiday. I thought she would be back by now. I was about to peel sweet potatoes to make a pie. Come on into the kitchen and keep me company."

James followed her to the kitchen. He stood watching her as she went to the cupboard, took a cup out, and filled it with coffee. She placed it on the table with sugar and cream. He pulled out a chair from the table, took a seat, and watched as she stood with her back to him, peeling sweet potatoes.

Without turning around, she spoke, "You didn't say anything about the Christmas tree."

He pretended like he didn't know why she said what she said, "It's a nice tree."

"Did you notice the tree topper? It's the star Robert made when we were in the third grade. Mom decided to decorate the tree with the decorations we made when we were kids."

"I noticed. So, has Rose mentioned Robert?"

"No. She just decorated the tree without saying a word. James, do you think Robert is dead?"

As he prepared to lie, the words of Shakespeare, quoted by Robert, echoed in his mind. To honor the promise he had made, he found himself on the brink of entering Robert's realm of deceit. "I'm not sure, Sarah. I hope he's still alive."

"Do you believe the rumors about him passing?"

"Sarah, I don't know what to believe."

"I don't either." She turned around to face him, "Well, tell me about your trip to Baltimore."

CHAPTER THIRTY-FOUR

Sarah

April 6, 1998. Love shattered the dark shadows that scarred her existence. Sarah was sixty-seven years old and still living at home with her mother. The only time she didn't live at home was when she was away in college. Love eluded her until now. She met John Peters just when she had accepted loneliness as her lifetime companion. She often asked herself why she was still at home with her mother and had not gotten married. Was it because she had not met the right person? Was it because Robert, in his note, had asked her to take care of their mother? Whatever the reason, it was now behind her. She was in love.

She had only three hours before she would be in John's arms. A long boring day of professional development. Listening to someone talking at her all day was more tiring than dealing with her students. At three thirty-one, Sarah was in her car. She smiled to herself as she drove through town. *It feels good to smile for no reason,* she thought. When she got home, Rose was sitting on the porch. Sarah kissed her on the cheek and ran into the house, showered, and packed an overnight bag.

As she was leaving, she paused at Robert's bedroom door. Setting her overnight bag down, she pushed the door open. The room remained untouched, a testament to Rose's refusal to alter anything. Sarah wandered the room, her fingers tracing the surfaces of the dresser, desk, and chair. Her gaze landed on a photo of her and Robert at a church picnic, his arm locked around her neck. A smile crossed her face as she approached her brother's bed and gently sat on its edge. Sarah often conversed with Robert in her thoughts. These mental dialogues ranged from chastising him for not revealing his departure to sharing her triumphs and sorrows. She frequently questioned him about the rumors swirling around him, and in her mind, his response was always consistent: "No, Sarah, I would never do such a thing."

She found solace in her imaginary dialogues. *"Robert, I've met someone who loves me. He makes me feel cherished, and I adore him. I believe you would approve of him. Robert, I need one thing from you. Please release me from the duty of caring for Mom."*

Before she could hear what she believed to be his reply, she glanced at her watch, jumped up, straightened out the bed, returned the picture to the dresser, and exited the room, gently closing the door. Pausing to hold the doorknob, she inhaled deeply, let go, and grabbed her overnight bag. Approaching the front door, she saw Rose on the porch, looking intently down the street. "Mom."

Startled, Rose spun around to face Sarah. "You scared me," she said. Her thoughts had been preoccupied with the note Charlie had left her, a note she kept secret from everyone, a note that constantly occupied her thoughts.

"Mom, are you alright?"

"Of course, I am. I was just thinking about your father." Pointing to the street, "He died … your father died right there. You know, no one was ever arrested."

"I know, Mama." Sarah felt guilty. She was on her way to meet the man she loved while her mother longed for the love she once had. "Do you want me to stay here with you?"

Rose looked at Sarah, "No, baby, no! I'm good. The past is the past, and that's where we need to leave it. Look at you! You look so pretty."

"Thank you. Mom don't wait up for me. I need to be at work for a seven-thirty meeting tomorrow morning, but I'll be back here tomorrow to go with you to your doctor's appointment."

Rose smiled at her. "You know I can go to the doctor by myself. Besides, when am I going to meet this man of yours?"

"I know, Mom, but the doctor requested my presence. And as far as when you'll meet John, soon. I think very soon."

"He must be special. It is so nice to see you smiling."

"Mom, I smile."

"Not often enough. Baby, you have such a pretty smile. I'm glad he makes you smile."

"Thanks, Mom. I love you."

"I love you too. Have fun. Hey, wait! What do you think the doctor will say to me tomorrow?"

Sarah could see that her mother was a bit bothered. "Mom, I don't know; but we'll know tomorrow."

"Do you think it's…?"

"Mom, stop worrying. Worrying doesn't change anything."

"You're right. Worrying doesn't change a thing, but I have nothing else to do, so I'll just sit here on the porch and worry." Rose laughed, "You go on now! Be safe."

"Mom, what am I going to do with you?" Sarah kissed her mother and left.

CHAPTER THIRTY-FIVE

Sarah

With the sunshine, the fog disappeared. Her newfound happiness with John was like a foggy morning. John was her sunshine. Sarah had only known him for four months, but something in her spirit told her he was the one.

She met him on the last day of school before Christmas vacation. It was Friday, so her mother would have fried fish, baked potato, and a salad waiting for her when she got home. She desired a solitary celebration, free from conversation. So, she made a reservation at The Royal Restaurant. It was one of her favorites. It was a bit pricey, so she only went there on special occasions.

A tall attractive blond hostess greeted Sarah with a smile. She directed Sarah to a seat by the fireplace. The lighting was dim.

Perfect! Just perfect, Sarah thought. The waiter, a slender young man with freckles and hazel eyes, pulled out the chair for her. After she sat down, he took her napkin and placed it on her lap.

"Hi, my name is Harrison. I will be your server. What can I get you to drink?"

"I will have a glass of your best Chardonnay."

After perusing the menu, Sarah stared at the flicking flames in the fireplace. She could feel the tension leaving her body. Harrison returned with her wine, a breadbasket, and olive oil.

"Are you ready to order?"

"Yes. I want to start with the escargot in garlicky butter, a cup of lobster bisque, the house salad, the Chilean Sea Bass, roasted Brussels sprouts, and Gorgonzola mac and cheese."

"Excellent selections."

Smiling, she thought, *there is no way I can eat all that food, but I will enjoy trying. I should've called Mom to tell her I wouldn't be there for dinner, but I needed my time. I love her, but I didn't want to have to answer any questions about why I wanted to have dinner alone.*

Harrison returned with her escargot. After he left, she picked up her seafood fork, pierced an escargot, and slowly put it in her mouth. Closing her eyes, she slowly chewed because she wanted to savor every morsel. She repeated this ritual until she had eaten them all. Then she broke a piece of the sourdough bread, dipped it in garlic butter, and repeated the ritual. This time, as she opened her eyes to tear off another piece of bread, she realized a man from a table across the restaurant was observing her. He offered a smile, his deep dimples visible even from a distance. Sarah averted his gaze, tore off another piece of bread, and began to butter it. She could tell from the corner of her eye that he was still looking. A sense of discomfort and irritation started to settle in. *I will say something to my waiter*, she thought. She shifted sideways in her chair and noticed the man leaving his seat. *Maybe he is going,* she thought. *No, he is coming over here. What the....*

"Hello. I was watching you from across the room."

"I know. Why?"

"You're alone. You're too pretty to be dining alone, so I decided to join you."

He settled into a chair at her table, his features sculpted and the color of rich chocolate, as if caressed repeatedly by the sun's rays.

Damn, was what she thought, but she said, *"Excuse me."*

"My name is John...."

She felt herself blushing. "I don't mean to be rude. But...."

Chuckling, he smiled, "Well, don't be."

"Don't be what?"

"Rude. You're alone, and I'm alone." He dropped his head like a child who had just been chastised. "If we dine together, they can use my table for other patrons."

"That is so thoughtful of you, but I...."

"Please, don't send me back to my table. I don't want to eat alone. Be nice." He smiled, showing his pretty white teeth. His deep dimples looked like small caverns.

"I don't know you."

"My name is John Peters."

Starting to feel a bit irritated, "Listen, I...."

He interrupted before she could complete her sentence, "Please, pretty lady, don't make me beg. I don't want to eat alone."

"Well, I did."

"Tell me, why would you want to eat alone."

She thought, *for the same reason you are eating alone. I want my time,* but she said, "Okay, Mr. Peters. You're relentless. My name is Sarah Franklin."

"Please, don't call me Mr. Peters. Call me John or Johnny."

"Okay, Mr. John, I won't send you back to your table. Please have a seat." They both laughed.

Four months had passed. As she neared John's apartment door, a wave of nervousness washed over her. The reason was unclear, but she sensed an impending event. Hesitating at the door, she almost turned to leave. *"Stop being foolish,"* she chided herself mentally. *"You've been alone too long. Happiness is overdue in your life."* With a deep, steadying breath, she composed herself, checked her appearance, and tapped lightly on the door. It swung open, revealing John's welcoming smile.

"Hi, beautiful."

Sarah stood there staring at him like it was her first time seeing him. He was wearing tight jeans and a white T-shirt. She loved his smile.

"Are you coming in, or are you going to stand out there all night?"

"Of course, I'm coming in."

He took her hand and pulled her into his apartment.

She giggled. "What are you cooking? Something smells good."

"It's me." He laughed.

"Let me see." Standing on her toes, she sniffed his face.

"I love you, Sarah Franklin." He leaned down to kiss her.

She put her index finger on his lips. "Do you? You have only known me for four months."

"Yes, I do. I fell in love with you the first moment I saw you. Now, my love, have a seat."

Despite the living room's masculine decor, she found it immensely comfortable. The brown leather sofa and loveseat exuded softness and warmth. A cherry wood coffee table stood before the sofa, adorned with a photo of the couple taken at a concert. Dark hardwood floors added depth to the space. The dining room, a continuation of the living room, featured a table set for two, with a solitary candle as its centerpiece. Their laughter and conversation filled the room during dinner. Post-dinner, they nestled into the sofa, finding solace in each other's embrace, before proceeding to the bedroom.

Sarah had to be at work early. She didn't want to wake him. She kissed him lightly on his luscious lips. She smiled to herself, thinking *he is the one. He has captured my heart. I am in love with this man. He's a good man.*

The air was fresh after last night's rain. Taking a deep breath, she laughed out loud. She hoped the meeting would be brief. She had to pick up her mother for her doctor's appointment. She didn't know how she would tell her mother John had asked her to move in with him.

A Mother's White Lie

CHAPTER THIRTY-SIX

Rose

April 7, 1998. The ability to forget the fear and pain brought by distressing news might be a blessing for some, yet for others, it could signal the end. Rose switched on her radio, and Tammy Wynette's "Stand by Your Man" filled the room. Gazing at her reflection in the mirror of her 1940s vintage dresser, Rose covered her mouth with her hands. Gradually, she moved her hands upwards, brushing away the tears welling in her eyes. She stood there, looking past her reflection to the image of her bed in the mirror. With a smile, she glanced down, gently stroking the smooth mahogany of the dresser. Turning towards the bed, she imagined him there with a red rose, smiling back at her. As if he were present, she spoke, "Charlie, do you remember after we dedicated ourselves to one another under the pear tree, we came upstairs and fell into one another's arms? You slowly removed my clothes, exciting everything in me. I have never known another man, but I can't imagine experiencing with anyone else the intensity of that night."

She crossed to the window, parted the curtains, and pulled up the shade. It rained all night, but the sun's warmth wrapped itself around the April morning like a blanket. The air smelled crisp and clean. At the song's end, the radio announcer's voice blasted, "It's Thursday, April 7, 1998; Tammy Wynette died last night in her Nashville, Tennessee home."

Rose shook her head and muttered, "Another death." She turned off the radio. Speaking aloud, "I've got to get ready. Where is Sarah? She promised she would be here to take me to my doctor's appointment."

A navy-blue A-line skirt and a white silk blouse were draped over Charlie's lounger. After his passing, that was the sole item she moved. Together with her son, Robert, she transferred it from the living room to a bedroom corner. It wasn't merely Charlie's chair; it was a shared haven. They had spent countless hours nestled in it. Those moments were filled with joy. Now, she would sit in it nightly before sleep, cherishing the memories of her days with Charlie.

Returning to the mirror, she removed the lid from a jar of moisturizer, dipped her finger in, and dotted her face with the cream. Rose massaged it softly into her copper-toned skin. Remarkably wrinkle-free for someone in her eighties, the signs of her years were most evident in the loose skin around her neck. Her sole cosmetic was a swipe of ruby red lipstick. She fashioned her silver, shoulder-length hair into a French roll, donned her blouse, and slid into her skirt. Dressed, she drew back the curtains, anticipation tinged with an inexplicable sense of dread embraced her as she awaited Sarah's return.

A Mother's White Lie

CHAPTER THIRTY-SEVEN

Rose and Sarah

Rose and Sarah were seated in front of a grand mahogany desk. Behind it, a vast picture window revealed a bird's nest cradled in the branches of an oak tree. Within, fledglings with gaping mouths awaited their next meal from their mama.

Anxiety clenched Rose's heart as she sat with her daughter in Dr. Freda Woodson's office. She ran her hands over her navy-blue skirt, ironing out non-existent creases. Dr. Woodson, a petite woman with honey-hued skin and auburn, cropped hair, entered with customary pleasantries: a warm 'good morning,' a friendly smile, and a firm handshake. It was a follow-up appointment; Rose had consulted Dr. Woodson two weeks earlier. She made an appointment to see the doctor because she felt stressed and couldn't understand why she was forgetting things – conversations, birthdays, names.

Even though Sarah had her reservations, she reassured her mother that there was no cause for concern. Sarah had convinced herself that memory lapses and feelings of anxiety were common aspects of aging.

Dr. Woodson leaned forward in her chair. "How are you feeling today, Rose?"

Rose smiled, "I'm fine. How're you doing, Dr. Woodson?"

"I can't complain." Looking from Rose to Sarah, Dr. Woodson asked, "Sarah, how are you doing?"

Sarah smiled and responded, "I'm fine, Dr. Woodson."

Shifting her eyes from Sarah to Rose, then back to Sarah, Dr. Woodson smiled, "I'm so glad you could come to this follow-up with your mother."

"It's no problem. She is my mom." Something about Dr. Woodson's demeanor made Sarah feel uncomfortable. Her eyes narrowed as she watched Dr. Woodson open the folder on her desk labeled Rose Franklin. The next words she heard tumbling into the air were the onset of Alzheimer's disease. Taking a deep breath and biting her bottom lip, Sarah reached for her mother's hand. Time stood still for a moment. No one said a word. The silence was broken when Sarah asked the doctor, "Are you sure?" A litany of other questions, from Sarah, followed that one question.

Rose felt the muscles in her body tense up. Her heart was beating so fast, it felt like it was trying to find an escape route out of her body. Consumed by her own thoughts, all Rose heard were the words "onset of Alzheimer's disease." *God, my biggest fear has become my reality. Reality! How much longer will I know what reality is? Why God, why? I've never feared getting old. My prayer has always been to let me grow old with dignity and in my right mind. I guess I can forget that. That's funny! I will be forgetting everything! How do I handle this? I've seen people with this disease. I've seen them disappear. I've seen them forget family members. Is that going to happen to me? Will I one day not know my daughter? How can you forget the babies you carried in your body for nine months? Alzheimer's! Death without dying! I've got to find a way to leave the memory of me that I am now; not the me I'll become.* Rose's thoughts were interrupted when Sarah touched her arm.

"Mom, Dr. Woodson is talking to you."

Startled by Sarah's touch, Rose's body jerked, "Huh?" Without any forewarning, a tear rolled down Rose's cheek. With her lower lip quivering, Rose whispered, "I'm sorry. I don't know where that came from." She wiped her tears away with her finger.

Reaching behind her desk, Dr. Woodson pulled out a Kleenex and leaned across her desk to hand it to Rose. She sat back in her chair, "I know this isn't something you wanted to hear. Do you have any questions?"

Rose took a deep breath. Dr. Woodson's words made her feel like someone was punching her in the stomach. Her voice trembled, "No ... No, I have no questions." Trying not to break, Rose put her hand over her mouth and uttered, "I just don't want to be a burden to anyone."

Clasping her mother's hand, Sarah gently patted it, offering reassurance that all would be well. "Mama, you won't be a burden," she said, attempting to stifle her fears by avoiding her mother's gaze and voicing the comfort she believed her mother needed.

Rose blinked to fight back tears, "I'm so sorry, baby. We both know what this disease will do. I don't want to forget."

"It'll be alright," Sarah said, trying to comfort her mother, while a whirlwind of thoughts invaded her mind. *But it's not going to be alright. How am I going to take care of her? I need to work.*

I want to work. I've never had my time. John … I can't allow myself to go there. I can't be selfish. I'm not ready for memories of me being wiped from my mother's mind. I'm not ready to have my mother ask me 'Do I know you?' I don't want to make all the decisions by myself. I need my brother. Sarah's thoughts of self were curbed when she heard Rose's voice.

"I'm so sorry, baby."

Dr. Woodson sat watching the two women as they tried to digest the diagnosis of Alzheimer's.

With a lump in her throat, Sarah asked, "Do I need someone to come in to be with her during the day?"

"I think she'll be fine for a while. You'll know when you'll need to make changes. I'll also help you when the time comes. I'm going to give you a prescription. It'll help, but it will not prevent it. I'll see you in a month. Please stop by the front desk, and one of the ladies will schedule your next appointment."

"Thank you, doctor." Sarah stood up. She leaned down to help her mother up by supporting her mother's elbow with her hand.

Rose snapped, "I can stand on my own, thank you."

"I'm sorry, Mom." They walked in silence out of the door of Dr. Woodson's office.

A Mother's White Lie

CHAPTER THIRTY-EIGHT

Sarah

Sarah never introduced her mother to John, nor did she inform her that John had invited her to move in with him. John called every day, but Sarah didn't respond. Her soul felt as if it had been eviscerated and left to dry on a fence. It had been three weeks since Rose's diagnosis, and three weeks of sleepless nights for Sarah. She experienced the same nightmare every night following Rose's doctor's visit. Tonight was no different. A shadowy figure adorned in black entered her bedroom. A black veil obscured the face. Sarah discerned Rose's face behind the lace veil as the figure neared. Her mother paused to gaze at her, standing silently. Then, she moved to the window and settled on the seat, turning away from Sarah. Rising from the bed, Sarah approached her. She inquired if her mother was alright but received no reply. When Sarah laid a hand on her mother's shoulder, the figure turned; it wasn't her mother, but Sarah herself, confronting her with a voice as grave as death, questioning, "Do I know you?" Sarah woke up trembling, her breaths coming as if she had just finished a ten-mile run. Her heart pounded as though it was trying to break free from her chest, and her mouth was as dry as a desert.

Attempting to gather her thoughts, she sat on the bed, weaving her fingers through her dense, wavy salt-and-pepper hair. The moonlight poured in through the window, casting a glow over the room. Sarah drew back the covers, settled on the bed's edge, and slid her feet into her slippers. Slowly standing, she walked over to an overstuffed chair by a full-length mirror to pick up her robe. As she put on her robe, she caught sight of herself in the mirror and stopped, wrapping her arms around herself. Overcome with thoughts of John, she felt her knees buckle, and she sank to the floor. Tears streamed down her face, expressing her silent sorrow, the loss of what could have been, her feelings of guilt, and the daunting prospect of caring for her mother. With a dry mouth and throat, she went to the kitchen for a drink, finding Rose at the table. The stark whiteness of the kitchen struck her—the enamel table, vinyl chairs, cupboards, and linoleum, all an unyielding white. Sarah paused in the doorway, watching her mother write, unnoticed by Rose. "Mom, are you alright?"

Startled, Rose let her pencil fall. She glanced at her daughter, shook her head, and chuckled. "You gave me a fright. But yes, I'm fine."

"What are you doing up?" Sarah asked.

She paused to take a sip of tea from the cup on the table, pondering for a moment. "I couldn't sleep. Why are you awake?"

Sarah was reluctant to share her nightmare with her mother. "I couldn't sleep either. What are you doing?"

"Come, sit down. I want to talk to you."

"Mom...."

"Please ... I just want you to listen. I need to put things in order."

"Mom, you don't have to worry about...."

"Please just listen! At some point, you won't be able to care for me. I'll have to be placed in an assisted living facility or a nursing home. However, this house will be okay because I put your name on the deed four years ago. Your name is also on all the other properties your father left me. Last week I visited several facilities. When the time comes, I want to be placed at Greener Pastures. It's not far from here, it's clean, the staff seems to respect the residents, and the grounds are beautiful. Now, if they don't have availability, when it is time for me to go into a facility, I have listed several others here."

"Mama, do we need to talk about this now?"

"Yes, we do. I only have a couple of demands."

"Demands? What are your demands?"

"When I go to Greener Pastures. I want a roommate. I don't want to be isolated. Do you understand?"

Not knowing what to say, Sarah replied, "Yes, ma'am."

"I don't want you to change anything in my room here at the house. If possible, I would like to die in my own bed. Even if you think I don't recognize it as my room, I feel there will be recognition and comfort somewhere in my spirit. Promise me you will leave my room as it is and try to bring me home when it's my time."

"I promise, Mom."

Sarah was not surprised by her mother's composure and self-control; it was not her first time observing it. She knew this had to be a difficult and trying time for her mother, but she also knew her mother had always kept a firm grip on her life.

Rose had not confided in her daughter about contemplating suicide, a thought she had only casted aside in the hope of seeing her son once more.

A Mother's White Lie

CHAPTER THIRTY-NINE

Sarah

May 2001. Death came slowly, but it came. It didn't cease her heartbeat; rather, it dimmed her mind and the recognition of her beloved ones. Over the following three years, the resilient woman who, despite not finishing school, had mastered managing finances, paying bills, maintaining a household, caring for her children, and handling the real estate bequeathed after her husband's death, began to fade into a stranger to Sarah. She seized every opportunity to express her love to her mother. She longed to phone her brother, wishing he could convey his love to their mother. The idea of hiring someone to locate him crossed her mind, but she dismissed it.

Sarah's life experienced a significant change. Releasing John from her life was the sole sacrifice she deemed necessary. Although work was not a necessity for her, Sarah couldn't bring herself to resign as it served as her solace. Consequently, she hired Lucy, a friend's daughter recommended by her Aunt Rachael. Lucy was slender, with a narrow face and bad skin, and though in her early thirties, she looked much older. She came every morning at six-thirty to ensure Rose didn't attempt to cook or skip her meals.

Tending to Rose was generally easier in the mornings than in the evenings. Upon returning from work, Sarah found Rose restless, pacing between rooms. At a medical appointment, Dr. Woodson informed Sarah that Rose's evening disorientation and restlessness were referred to as sundowning.

One evening when Sarah came home from work, she found two police cars in front of the house. *Oh my God! What has happened to my mother?* She prepared herself for the worst as she got out of her car. Lucy met her before she got to the porch.

"I'm sorry, Miss Sarah. I was in the...."

Frantically she asked, "Lucy, what's going on? Why are you out here? Is my mom alright? Where is she?"

"While I was using the bathroom, your mom called 911. After the fifth call, two police cars were sent out to investigate."

"Five calls!"

Lucy followed behind Sarah, sobbing, "I'm so sorry! I needed to use the bathroom. When I came out of the bathroom, she was sitting on the sofa with the telephone in her hands. I took the telephone from her and put it back on the hook. Then I heard this loud banging on the door. When I opened the door, three policemen were standing there. They told me they had received five 911 calls. Miss Sarah, I didn't know she had called 911 until I opened the door. They told me someone called to report a murder and a child missing. I explained the situation as best as I could. They said they would stay until you got home."

Sarah was trembling. "It's alright, Lucy. You can go home."

"Yes, ma'am. I'm sorry." Lucy walked away, mumbling apologies.

Sarah rushed through the front door. "What's going on? Is my mom alright?" She could hear Rose yelling. Sarah's heart felt like it was in her throat.

"No! No! My husband was murdered! Right out in front of this house. You need to find out who did it! Please find the person who murdered my husband."

"Mom! Mom!"

A tall redheaded policeman with a face covered with freckles met Sarah outside the living room door. Tipping his hat, "Hi, ma'am. I'm Officer Michael O'Riley. Your mother is alright. We are trying to calm her down. We can't get her to stay in just one spot. She called 911, saying her husband had been murdered and her son was missing. By the time we got here, she had made four more calls. We were dispatched out to investigate what was going on."

He moved aside, allowing Sarah to enter the living room, then positioned himself in the doorway. As Sarah stepped into the room, she noticed a female officer and her male counterpart. The female officer, slender with a short bob of brown hair, was standing at the center of the room. The male officer, whose dark hair and joined eyebrows framed his face, was seated. Both officers observed Rose as she paced. Noticing Sarah, the male officer promptly rose to his feet.

Sarah approached her mother, "Mom, Mom, are you alright?"

Hearing Sarah's voice, Rose stood still. She smiled, "Good, Sarah, you are home. These nice people came by to see me."

The male officer in the living room spoke, "Good evening, ma'am. I'm Officer Brian Jackson." Pointing to the female officer, "This is Officer Mary Stephens." He then turned to the officer standing in the doorway.

Before he could say anymore, Officer O'Reilly spoke, "I've already introduced myself."

Officer Jackson nodded to Officer O'Reilly. He turned to Sarah, "Are you her daughter?"

Standing before her mother, Sarah reached out to take her mother's hand. "Yes. My name is Sarah Franklin."

Officer Stephens explained, "Your mother said your brother is missing, and her husband was murdered."

"My brother left home when he was eighteen years old. That was fifty-plus years ago. My father was killed by a hit-and-run driver in 1940. They never found out who did it."

Officer Stephens nodded, "Lucy explained the situation, but we stayed to verify everything. Ma'am, she called 911 five times. You know she can't do that."

"Thank you. I know. She has been getting upset in the evenings for the last few weeks. I am so sorry. This is the first time she has done something like this. I will call her doctor tomorrow morning."

Officer O'Reilly interjected, "I believe we've covered everything. Have a pleasant evening, and don't hesitate to contact us if you need any further assistance."

As Sarah watched the officers enter their patrol cars, she could hear Dr. Woodson's voice in her mind; *you will know when it's time.*

CHAPTER FORTY

Sarah and Rose

The night had stretched long, and the day promised to stretch even longer. Rose was agitated, pacing the house until dawn. When Sarah finally soothed her mother into bed, the birds were already heralding the new day. It had been two weeks since the emergency calls. Descending the stairs, Sarah noticed a squeak in the second step from the top for the first time. Careful not to wake Rose, she shifted her weight from the noisy step, gripping the banister. Reaching the bottom, she tidied the living room, gathering the cushions Rose had scattered in her nocturnal restlessness. In the kitchen, Sarah prepared the coffee maker, spooning in two generous measures of coffee, adding water, and switching on the machine.

Sarah flung the kitchen door open, seeking the fresh air's revitalizing embrace. She watched the squirrels' energetic antics around the pear tree, a symbol of her parents' enduring love. Their story, deeply ingrained in her memory, was told time and again. The world around her had shifted; laws had changed. If her father had lived, he could have legally married her mother. People might stay the same, but laws do not. It was the aroma of coffee that brought her back to reality.

As she poured herself a cup of coffee and took a seat at the table, Sarah's thoughts drifted back to the night she discovered Rose in the kitchen, planning for the time when she would no longer be able to manage her own affairs. She recalled her attempts to dissuade Rose, unwilling to confront the possibility of her mother not recognizing her. Now, she appreciated that Rose had planned for the inevitable day she couldn't stay at home. Following the emergency calls, Sarah had discussions with Rose's physician and the head of Greener Pastures. They had set a date and time for Rose to move from her cherished home to Greener Pastures. Sarah understood that she would be unable to visit for the first two weeks after her mother settled into the home, allowing Rose a period to adjust.

The day had arrived. Clasping her mother's hand, Sarah entered her new home with Rose. The building was bright and bathed in light, yet it lacked an aura of joy. The scents and noises were nothing like those of home.

Holding tightly to her mother's hand, she felt tears bubbling up from her gut. She fought them back because this was not the time for tears. She knew what she had to do. At that moment, she wished she had her mother's resolve.

Sarah caught a glimpse of the community room. Several people were sitting expressionless. *This is my mom's future.* She felt sadness wash over her. *Why do they call this place Greener Pastures? I don't see this place offering a better life than the life people had before coming here. This place is the last mile before the end. Maybe they call it Greener Pastures because they transition to a greener pasture from here. I need to stop trying to analyze things. This is Mom's choice.*

All at once, Sarah sensed her mother attempting to withdraw. Puzzled by her mother's actions, Sarah's hold grew firmer. She questioned whether Rose was aware of their surroundings. Unable to release her hand, Rose began guiding Sarah toward the baby grand piano in the community room. As Sarah caught sight of the piano, her grip relaxed.

Rose walked over to the piano. She stood staring. Her fingers timidly touched the keys. "Charlie ... Charlie bought this for me."

"Yes, Mom, Daddy bought you a piano."

Looking around to see who was watching, Sarah gently put her arms around her mother. "No, Mom. Come on. I want to show you your room."

"My room?"

"Yes. Come on."

Rose allowed Sarah to guide her down an extensive hallway, pausing at the last room. Despite Sarah's promise to her mother to avoid isolation, she desired privacy for her, thus choosing a single-occupancy room. Sarah decorated the room with framed photographs of her father, brother, and herself, and placed her mother's favorite chair by the window overlooking the rose garden.

Sarah guided her mother to a chair. As Rose took a seat, Sarah knelt before her. "Mom, do you like this room? See, there's a rose garden. And with a television and a telephone here, you won't feel lonely," she said. Sarah sought to comfort herself, affirming that her decision was correct, even though it contradicted her mother's wishes.

Rose sat, with her head bowed, looking at her lap.

Sarah fought to keep her thoughts at bay, yet the prospect of leaving her mother was daunting. She was suddenly overwhelmed by a surge of guilt. Tears welled up in her eyes. She knelt beside her mother's chair, laying her head in her lap, and whispered, "Mom, I'm sorry. You know I love you."

In a fleeting moment, Rose's eyes seemed to flicker with recognition. She gently stroked Sarah's face, wiping away her tears. Sarah looked at her mother, her eyes filled with love, fear, and compassion. Standing up from her mother's lap, she kissed her mother's forehead and left.

CHAPTER FORTY-ONE

Rose

She noticed faint shadows and heard soft moans and cries seeping under the door sills. Sleep did not feature in Rose's nightly routine at Greener Pastures. With doors shut and lights dimmed, Rose meandered through the hallways. The night staff knew of her nocturnal strolls. Invariably, she was drawn to the baby grand piano during these escapades. Occasionally, the night staff would pause outside the community room, captivated as she played and, at times, sang. Unlike some residents, Rose's wanderings were harmless. Roughly an hour later, she would always return to her room.

During her fourth evening at Greener Pastures, Rose perched on the piano bench, shoulders curved inward. Her fingers danced lightly over the piano keys. She sensed a hand gently resting on her back as she paused to shift her position on the bench.

"Keep playing."

Twisting slightly on the bench, she saw Sidney Schmitt, in navy blue pajamas, smiling down at her. Sidney was a nonagenarian, but he looked to be in his seventies. When he was younger, he stood six feet five inches. Age had hunched him over. He had been at Greener Pastures for two years. His hand moved in a circular motion on Rose's back. Then he sat beside her on the bench.

Rose smiled. "Charlie…Charlie, I am so glad to see you."

Sidney rubbed his chin with his thin white fingers. "Please play some more."

"I don't want to, Charlie."

Sidney didn't bother to tell her his name was not Charlie.

CHAPTER FORTY-TWO

Sarah

The first night after Sarah left her mother at Greener Pastures, she found no sleep. Lying in bed, she gazed at the shadows dancing on the wall, cast by the moonlight seeping through the curtains. The house was quiet. Too quiet. She half-expected to hear her mother's footsteps pacing the floor. Wrapping the covers tighter around her neck, she chuckled and mumbled, *"I don't have to struggle anymore with trying to get her into bed. I don't have to fix breakfast. I don't have to try to make Mom eat. I don't have to worry about what she is doing. I don't have to...."* She suddenly stopped and asked herself, "What is my purpose now?" She felt a profound sense of solitude. Anger joined her in bed, a companion fueled by the sacrifices she made caring for her mother. Anger caressed her because she had a brother who should be sharing the responsibility for their mother's care, but she didn't know where he was. Anger seeped into her spirit because the mother she knew was breathing, but she was dead. Her anger dissolved into self-pity and she covered her face with her pillow to mute her cries.

* * *

A veil of tranquility enveloped the house. She reflected on how swiftly the past two weeks had elapsed. As she opened the kitchen door, a deep breath filled her lungs with the crisp morning breeze. With a robust cup of black coffee in hand, she settled in a spot that offered a view of the playful squirrels in the yard. A smile graced her face as she basked in newfound peace and the sharp taste of her coffee. Her eyes briefly met the funeral home calendar on the wall, where days and nights had merged indistinguishably. Today, she was to meet her mother, uncertain of what awaited her.

On her way to Greener Pastures, she vowed nothing would disturb the tranquility of her spirit. She repeatedly sang *Peace Be Still* until the elevator doors at Greener Pastures opened. Stepping out of the elevator, Sarah heard the words *by and by Lord, when the morning. All the saints of God gather home. We will tell the story of how we overcome. We'll understand it better by and by.* Sarah stood for a moment listening. She realized it was her mother's voice. *She is singing. Mom is singing.* Her mother's voice led her to the community room door, where she saw her mother sitting on the piano bench, playing, and singing. Sarah stood in the doorway watching. Beside her mother, on the bench, was a slender elderly man with a head full of short silver curls. He had his arm around her mother's waist. His feeble hand trembled as it moved from her waist to her upper back. Sarah wondered, *Who is he? Why is he so familiar with my mother? Why is she allowing him to put his hands on her like that?* Sarah stood speechless, watching the feeble hand moving back and forth. She didn't know why, but it made her feel uncomfortable. She didn't know what to do. Although the community room was filled with other residents, she felt like she had walked in on an intimate moment. Just as she was about to turn to leave, she felt a hand on her left shoulder. Mrs. Jefferson, the director of Greener Pastures, was smiling at her. "Hello, Sarah."

"Hi. Who is the man sitting with my mom?" Sarah's voice tinged with indignation.

Touching Sarah's arm to assure her Rose was safe, "Oh, that's Sidney. He has been here at Greener Pastures for a little over two years. His son comes to see him every day. He and your mother seem to enjoy one another's company. She calls him Charlie, and he doesn't seem to mind."

"Charlie was my dad."

"After you left, Rose wouldn't leave her room for activities for the first two days. Somehow, I don't know how, but Sidney and Rose found each other. They are now inseparable. They both seem so much happier."

From that day, whenever Sarah visited her mother, she also visited with Sidney. She liked Sidney and his son Donald.

A Mother's White Lie

CHAPTER FORTY-THREE

Sarah

November 2022. Sarah stood by her bedroom window, gazing outward. The world was tranquil, the rooftops blanketed in frost. Suddenly, she burst into song, "Chestnuts roasting on an open fire, Jack Frost nipping at your nose." Laughter spilled from her as she turned away from the window and descended the stairs. Casting a glance towards Robert's room, she vowed to let nothing disturb her peace today. She had honored her mother's wish to keep everything in her bedroom unchanged. Robert's door remained closed. She would occasionally enter both rooms to dust; other than that, they stayed untouched, relics of a bygone era. The silence of the house was therapeutic. Finally, she felt ready to concentrate on her own life. Since John, she hadn't allowed another man to get close. Her life had revolved around her work and her mother. John had ceased trying to reach out to her. She found out he had married and settled in Durham, North Carolina.

Sitting on the piano bench, she glided her fingers across the ivory and ebony keys, thoughts of her brother enveloping her. Robert shared Rose's fervor for music. A gentle smile touched Sarah's lips as she reminisced about composing tunes with Robert, who possessed the extraordinary gift of playing any melody perfectly after hearing it just once.

Now, she could search for the part of her that was missing: Robert. She had shared everything with him, believing he had done the same. They had been each other's guardians. Although Sarah was more accepted during their elementary years, there were moments when they both endured the harshness of childhood cruelty. Some classmates from Black Bottom would taunt, "Here come night and day, blackie and whitie, Sambo and Yellow Bone, the mongrel, and the half-breed." Their usual retort to such insults was, "Sticks and stones may break my bones, but words will never hurt me." Yet, the truth was, words did hurt.

United, they bore their anguish and wept in private. It was a sorrow beyond their father's understanding, and their mother's only counsel was to 'ignore it.' Yet, how could they disregard something so intricately woven into the fabric of their everyday existence?

Playing what she could remember of Twinkle, Twinkle Little Star, she thought, *I can hire a private investigator to locate Robert, but what if the rumors are true? Would he want to see me? Maybe he is dead. No, I can't think like that, but what if the rumors are true? Will I be able to forgive him? Was he ashamed of us? It's like he stepped off the edge of the earth.* Her thoughts were interrupted by the telephone ringing. Clutching the telephone to her ear "Hello," smiling, she said, "I've missed you."

CHAPTER FORTY-FOUR

James and Sarah

The sun was setting when he arrived. "Come in. It's cold out there. I was so glad to hear your voice. Why haven't you been home?"

"I don't know. You know how busy life can be."

James had not been home because he didn't like pretending. After seeing Robert in Baltimore, James didn't visit Sarah or his sister often. But he had kept in touch with Robert.

Sarah threw her arms around James. "You need to visit more often. Take your coat off and come on in the kitchen."

He took his coat off, draped it over the banister, and followed her to the kitchen.

"Sit down; take a load off." She went to the cupboard and took down two glasses.

Opting for the back door, he was distracted by a rustle near the pear tree, which triggered fond memories of hide-and-seek games with Sarah and Robert, with the pear tree serving as their home base. He was so immersed in his nostalgia that he didn't notice Sarah standing quietly behind him. "James."

When he heard his name, he turned to see her outstretched arm handing him a glass of lemonade. He smiled and took it, "Thank you!" He pulled out the chair at the end of the table. Sitting down, he placed his glass on the table.

She lifted her glass from the counter and rested against the sink, her gaze fixed on him. "I'm so relieved you're here. There's something I need to discuss with you." "What's up?"

"Well, you know Mom is at Greener Pastures. She has very few days or moments when her thoughts are clear. I think Robert should be here. I was thinking of hiring a private investigator to find Robert. What do you think?"

"I don't know. Why are you thinking about doing something like that now?"

"I thought it might help Mom if she saw him."

"I don't know, Sarah. When I visit with Rose, she doesn't know who I am."

"It was just a thought."

CHAPTER FORTY-FIVE

Sarah

August 2003. Many things were beyond Sarah's control. Five months had passed since Rose and Sidney were discovered together in bed. Sarah wanted help but had abandoned the thought of finding Robert. Each day began with her reflection in the mirror, reciting, *"God, grant me the serenity to accept the things I cannot change, the courage to change the things I can, and the wisdom to know the difference."* She clung to these words for strength, particularly today. The extent of pain caused by her mother's Alzheimer's had caught her off guard. The disease had robbed her of her mother. Occasionally, Rose remembered she had a daughter, yet she did not recognize Sarah. Acceptance had become Sarah's reality—accepting that the mother she once knew was gone, accepting the need to reintroduce herself to her mother daily, and accepting that her mother's joy was independent of hers. All Sarah desired was happiness for both her mother and her.

Once dressed, Sarah proceeded to the kitchen. As she measured out coffee grounds, she paused at the counter to gaze through the window at the backyard. She then filled the pot with coffee, switched it on, and settled at the kitchen table, absorbing the rhythmic sounds of the coffee dripping. Soon, the rich scent of brewing coffee enveloped the room. She stepped through the back door with a freshly poured cup in hand. The sun shyly emerged from a cloud cover, and the mingling fragrances of coffee and crisp morning air invigorated her senses. Chickadees danced in the sky, playfully chasing each other, while Sarah observed two butterflies in a delicate ballet. Her thoughts drifted to her mother's fate, contingent on the outcome of the impending meeting with Sidney's son, Donald.

I don't understand why Donald would not want his father to be happy. Sidney and Mom were happy when they found each other. Who cares if they were having sex? Who was it hurting? Sarah laughed out loud. *I'm envious. My Mama with Alzheimer's is getting more action than I am.* Cradling the coffee cup with both hands, she brought it to her lips and began to speak with God. *Father,* when *Donald caught Mom and his father in bed together, he acted like he had caught his teenage son in bed with a young girl. He just has to understand. He has to care. God, let this be a good day.*

As she sipped her coffee, a squirrel darting up the pear tree caught her eye. She longed to spend the day savoring her coffee and watching the wildlife, but it wasn't possible. Sarah took one last deep breath of the fresh morning air before closing the door. After rinsing her cup and setting it in the sink, she mustered a smile and exited the kitchen, to prepare to embrace the unchangeable.

CHAPTER FORTY-SIX

Greener Pastures

August 2003. The community room was bustling. In the center, Karen, seated in her wheelchair, sang *Somebody needs you, Lord, come by here. Somebody needs you, Lord, come by here.* With hands clasped behind her, Faye paced her usual route, scrutinizing each person's face as she passed by. Emily was sitting with George, yelling she couldn't hear. George desperately tried to reassure her nothing was being said for her to hear. By the window, Rose sat in her wheelchair, head bowed, as sunbeams streaming through the glass crowned her head. Feeling unusually well, Denise stopped to speak to Brittney and Bessie, who were seated at a table near the door.

"Hello, girls; what are you up to today?" Denise pulled out a chair.

Scratching her head, Bessie asked, "What day is it?"

Looking at her through squinted eyes, Denise cocked her head to one side and asked, "Why?"

Brittney looked from Bessie to Denise and said, "Let me see, what was the second egg choice at breakfast this morning?

Sitting down, Denise asked, "What does that have to do with the price of coffee?"

"Bessie asked what the day was."

Frustrated, Denise responded with an emphatic, "So?"

Brittney asked, "Why are you upset? I usually know what day it is by the second egg choice. Poached eggs are the first egg choice and are offered daily. The second egg choice breakdown: Sunday is scrambled eggs; Monday is cheesy eggs; Tuesday is fried eggs; Wednesday is breakfast casserole with eggs; Thursday is hard-boiled eggs; Friday is omelet; and Saturday is what they call breakfast scramble."

Bessie finally said, "I didn't eat eggs this morning."

Brittney looked at her and said, " I didn't either."

Trying to compose herself, Denise yelled, "Who gives a damn?"

Glancing around the room to see if people were looking at them, Bessie said in almost a whisper, "Denise, you asked what we were doing today. I was trying to determine what day it is so I could answer your question."

Laughing and shaking her head, Denise said, "I really don't care what you're doing. I was just being polite. We're probably all doing the same damn thing – NOTHING!"

Brittney frowned and asked, "Denise, why must you be so mean?"

Just as Denise was about to answer Brittney, Richard entered looking quite debonair, wearing grey slacks, a black fitted tee shirt, and walking with a cane. "Good morning, ladies. May I join you?"

Denise said, "Yes, as long as you don't ask what we're doing today."

Brittney and Bessie laughed.

As Richard pulled a chair out to sit, Denise said, "You look nice today. How are you doing?"

"I'm fine," Richard replied, smiling.

Bessie giggling like a schoolgirl, said, "Yes, you are."

Denise looked at Bessie, scowling, "Bessie, keep your draws on!"

"I'm just being truthful."

"Amen!" Tears of laughter were streaming down Brittney's face.

Bowing his head like a teenage boy, "Thank you, ladies. You are making me blush." When he raised his head, he saw Rose sitting with her head bowed. "Ladies, is Rose alright?"

All heads turned toward Rose sitting in front of the huge picture window.

"She is dying from heartbreak," Denise replied.

"Yes," agreed Bessie.

"So sad," said Brittany.

"Heartbreak?" Richard questioned.

"Janie Ruth hasn't told you about Rose?" Denise asked.

"When I asked her about Rose, she told me she would tell me about it later. Later never came." Richard declared.

"Where is Janie Ruth?" asked Bessie.

"I don't know. I haven't seen her this morning." Richard replied.

Denise straightened herself as much as she could in her chair. She cleared her throat.

"Well, after Rose got here, she and Sidney took a liking to one another. And…."

Richard interrupted, asking, "Who is Sidney?"

"Don't interrupt! Be patient!" Denise declared. "I'm getting to that. Sidney was here before Rose got here. I understand they met while wandering the halls when they should have been in their rooms. Once the staff knew what was happening, they kept an eye on them. Because Rose and Sidney seemed happy, the staff didn't see the harm in them meeting in the community room at night." Denise pointed to the baby grand piano in the room. "Rose would come in here at night to play the piano. We heard that Sidney came in one night while she was playing, and the rest is history."

Bessie blurted, "Don't forget, Rose doesn't call Sidney by his name. She calls him Charlie."

"Charlie?" asked Richard.

"Yes!" said Brittney.

"I'm telling this story!" declared Denise. "Let me do it my way. Sidney didn't seem to mind Rose calling him Charlie. He probably doesn't even know his name. Now, it's my understanding Charlie was Rose's husband's name. Well, he wasn't her husband. He was a white man, and you know, back then, it was against the law for Blacks and whites to marry each other. I swear, it's so hard to believe you couldn't love who you wanted to love." Denise chuckled and shook her head. "I guess it's not that hard to believe. It's happening to Rose all over again, but it's killing her this time. Now, where was I? Yes, Rose loved playing the piano. Well, it seemed Rose was doing more than playing the piano, and Sidney was doing more than listening."

Richard asked, "What do you mean?"

Denise glared at Richard.

He held up his hands, saying, "I'm sorry. I won't interrupt again."

"Better not!" declared Denise.

Brittney and Bessie giggled.

"As I was saying, Rose was doing more than playing the piano, and Sidney was doing more than listening. Sidney and Rose were sneaking into one another's rooms and having fun under the sheets."

Richard said, "I know I promised not to interrupt, but are you saying Sidney and, uh, Rose were having sex?"

"Yes, Richard, that is what I'm saying. One of the aides caught Rose giving Sidney a blow job."

Richard's jaw tightened. He squirmed in his seat.

Denise asked, "Richard, are you alright?"

Clearing his throat, "Yes. I didn't expect…. I'm just a bit shocked."

"Why? Just because you're old doesn't mean you're dead. Don't you still have sexual desires?"

Richard squirmed even more, "I…I…."

"Never mind your desires. Let me finish telling you the story. The director informed Rose's daughter and Sidney's son about what had happened. Sidney's son was really upset about the situation. The staff tried keeping Rose and Sidney apart, but Donald, Sidney's son, decided to move Sidney to another facility. I think he thought the sex would cause his father to have a heart attack. If that had happened, at least Sidney would have died with a smile." Denise giggled. "Anyway, since Sidney left, Rose has been slowly withering away. It's like her will to live left when Sidney left."

Quietly, Bessie said, "So sad."

Looking in Rose's direction, Richard was fighting the lump forming in his throat.

A Mother's White Lie

CHAPTER FORTY-SEVEN

Greener Pastures

The sun had ceased its peeking from behind the clouds. Sarah stood at the entrance of Greener Pastures, gripping the door handle. She took a moment to draw in a deep breath of the fresh air, savoring the inhalation and exhalation before stepping inside. Entering a code into the elevator, she pressed the button for the second floor. As the elevator ascended, Karen's voice, singing *"By and by, Lord, when the morning comes,"* reached her ears. The doors slid open, and she found herself face-to-face with Faye. They exchanged smiles and nods of acknowledgment. Sarah exited the elevator and started walking towards her mother's room. Faye followed closely behind her. Halfway down the hallway, Faye began mumbling. "Community room, community room."

Sarah halted suddenly, causing Faye to almost stumble over her heels. Then, Sarah turned around.

"Hello, Faye. Are you trying to tell me my mother is in the community room?"

Faye's smile conveyed agreement, prompting Sarah to head toward the community room with Faye trailing behind, echoing her steps. Upon their arrival, they were greeted by a hive of activity. Denise, Bessie, and Janie Ruth were at a table, engaged in a lively card game. Rose occupied a chair positioned to offer a clear view of everyone entering the room.

Taking a deep breath, Sarah walked toward her mother. *Is she smiling? Yes. She is smiling.* "Mom?"

"Hi, Sarah. You came to see me."

Her heart fluttered with joy. Her mother recognized her. "Yes, Mom. I come to see you every day."

"You do?"

"Yes, ma'am." Sarah sat on the arm of the chair. She reached for Rose's hand. "Mom, you know who I am."

"Of course, I know who you are. Charlie is coming."

"I don't know, Mom. I asked his son to bring him to see you. Are you comfortable?"

"Sarah, how does my hair look?"

"It looks alright. I'll just brush it a bit for you." The last time Rose recognized Sarah as her daughter was two months ago. Standing, Sarah rummaged through her pocketbook. She found a brush. She missed her mother. *God, what can I do to keep her here with me?* She brushed Rose's thinning silver hair. "Mom, you are so beautiful."

"Who are you?"

Oh no! Not now, God. Please, not now. God, how can you be so cruel? She inhaled and responded, "I'm your daughter, Sarah."

"You're not my Sarah!"

Crumbling to the floor, Sarah lightly patted Rose's hand while fighting back tears. "It's alright, Mom."

Rose pulled her hand away from Sarah's touch. "Don't touch me. Who are you?"

At that moment, Donald, Sidney's son, entered the community room. His tall, slender frame moved with purpose. Noticing Sarah on the floor next to Rose, he hesitated, dreading the impending conversation. Nonetheless, he approached, positioning himself behind her before speaking. "Hi, Sarah."

Startled, she pulled herself from the floor. Sarah was glad to have a reason not to feel like a little girl whose mother had just disowned her. "Oh, hi, you came."

Adjusting the sunshades he had rested on his head, he replied, "I said I'd be here. I assumed we'd meet in your mother's room. You could have informed me of your whereabouts. When I got off the elevator, I learned you were in the community room." Donald never planned to let his father see Rose again. He questioned why he had even made the effort to come.

Meanwhile, Sarah was thrilled at the prospect of her mom seeing Sidney. Initially, the community room was not her choice, but she explained, "I chose it because all of us should visit together, so no one feels isolated." Scanning the area for Sidney, Sarah inquired, "Where's your father? Is he already in Mom's room waiting for us?"

"I didn't bring him."

Disappointed, Sarah asked, "Why?"

"He's adjusting well to New Horizons, and I just felt a visit with your mother wouldn't be good."

"But you said...."

Irritated, Donald's voice was amplified. Unable to contain his frustration, he retorted, "I know what I said."

The raised intonation of Donald's voice captured the attention of Janie Ruth, Denise, and Bessie, who were engrossed in a card game. They paused their game to listen. Richard was on the verge of entering the community room when the voices reached his ears. He considered leaving but chose to sit on the bench outside the door instead.

Disappointed with himself for his tone and response to why he had not brought his father, Donald quietly said, "Let's try to be civil."

"Donald, please have a seat." Sarah turned to see who was looking.

"No, thank you. I am not staying." Donald turned to leave.

Sarah begged Donald. "Please don't go." Sarah could see Janie Ruth, Bessie, Brittney, and Denise trying to busy themselves with their cards, so it appeared they weren't listening. She looked back at Donald and said, "I understand your concern for your father."

"Well, if you understand...."

"Listen, Donald, I'm concerned about my mother. I love my mother just as much as you love your father."

Donald asked sarcastically, "Then why are we having this conversation?"

Rose smiled and whispered as though she was sharing a secret, "Charlie! Charlie is coming today."

She gazed at her mother, and a wave of sadness engulfed Sarah. Turning to Donald, she no longer minded the onlookers or eavesdroppers. Fighting tears, she implored him, "Look at her!

Just look at her! She may not recognize me, but she's been calling for your father since he left."

"I'm sorry."

Her tears morphed from sadness to anger. Sarah attempted to rein in her fury, speaking in hushed, measured tones. "Are you?" she questioned, the words she yearned to unleash clamoring within her. She shivered as if chilled to the bone. "If you truly cared, you wouldn't have moved your father. Who were they harming? They were content." Her gaze fixed on Donald, seeking a glimpse of humanity in someone she now deemed soulless.

Raising his arms in frustration, "It wasn't appropriate."

Sarah calmly asked, "Is it appropriate for you?"

Donald's face flushed red, and his eyes narrowed. "That's none of your business," he retorted. "Besides, I'm not ninety-five."

Striving to stay composed and to reach his compassionate side, she said, "I apologize. It was wrong of me to ask that. But they are in love, Donald. Can't you see that?"

At that moment, Lillie entered the community room, piercing the quiet of the attentive residents. She shuffled her walker towards Donald. "Cigars, cigarettes, Tiparillos."

Despite having encountered Lillie on each visit to Greener Pastures to see his father, Donald gazed at her as if she were a creature from an uncharted world. "What?"

Janie Ruth rose from her seat. She limped towards Lillie. "Not now, Lillie." But Lillie was stubborn; she refused to be ushered away. Janie Ruth nearly toppled over in her effort to steer Lillie elsewhere. "Damn it! Lillie, come on! Not now!"

Lillie hunched her shoulders. She followed Janie Ruth to the table where Bessie and Denise sat gazing with their mouths open. Faye was pacing back and forth at the other end of the community room, repeating "Hey honey, hey honey, what's going on here?"

Despite his reluctance, Donald attempted to regain his focus. "Love.... There is nothing wrong with being in love, but they were having sex. My father is too old for that. He has a bad heart. I have power of attorney and the right to decide what is best for him."

"What's best for him or what's best for you? I would think you would be happy if your father had found someone he wanted to spend time with – someone who made him feel happy, loved, and alive. Your father is in love with my mother, and she is in love with him. He declared his love for her in front of everybody."

Bessie yelled out, "He did do that."

Denise yelled, "Shut up, Bessie! We don't have a damn thing to do with this!"

The community room was becoming chaotic. Frustrated and embarrassed, Donald said, "I'm leaving. Good luck with your mother."

Rose, who hadn't stood by herself since Sidney's departure from Greener Pastures, rose to her feet and unleashed a blood-curdling scream, "Charlie!" Her scream took everyone by surprise. Donald stood still, petrified. Rose began to falter. Sarah quickly caught her mother in her embrace.

Several confused aides jumped up. A sudden silence enveloped the turmoil. Donald's heart thumped in his throat. He observed Sarah soothing her mother and helping her sit down again. His intention wasn't to inflict distress. Unsure of his next move, Donald began to walk toward the exit. Sarah chased him, halting him before Richard, sitting on the bench, with his head down. Both were unaware of Richard's presence.

Grabbing Donald's arm, Sarah pleaded with him. "Have a heart, please. Your father and my mother gave each other a reason for wanting to open their eyes in the mornings and breathe. That should mean something to you! My mother loved playing the piano and having your father sing to her."

"Your mother doesn't even know my father's name. She thinks he is her dead husband. There's no need to talk about this any longer. I'm not going to change my mind. I'm not sacrificing my father's well-being for your mother."

Sarah looked on as Donald vanished through the doors at the corridor's end. Making her mother's final days joyful was crucial to her, yet she felt powerless to alter the course of events.

Amused by what had just transpired, Denise chuckled and whispered, "After listening to all that commotion, I'm going to have a sexual power of attorney drawn up tomorrow. I need to do it while I'm still in my right mind because I don't want my children blocking me saying I can't get a little bit because they have power of attorney."

Janie Ruth looked at Denise and shook her head. "Shut up! Right mind? You must be joking. You don't even have a mind."

CHAPTER FORTY-EIGHT

James

Being the guardian of a secret, he was aware that eventually, the truth would emerge. It was unavoidable, yet his daily prayer was for that day not to come. James had moved back to Lynchburg recently to be closer to his sister, Sarah, and Robert, who had also returned to Lynchburg. He found it surprising that Sarah and Robert had not crossed paths yet.

The sky was a blanket of grey, and the distant rumble of thunder was audible. He mused that *where there's thunder, lightning surely follows.* Pouring a shot of bourbon, he took a sip, feeling the warmth spread through him. With a smile, he acknowledged the day's pleasantness. He placed his drink beside the telephone on the end table, adjacent to his favored chair. Settling into the chair, he shed his shoes and propped one foot on the hassock. As he was about to raise his other foot, the phone's ring halted him. "This had better be worth it," he grumbled. Removing his foot from the hassock, he picked up the receiver and held it to his left ear. "Hello?" he answered. The voice on the line brought a frown of confusion, knitting his brows as he listened, his heart thumping louder with each second.

"Okay. Good-bye." He placed the receiver back in the cradle. "Damn!" He reached for his glass and gulped down the remaining bourbon in one swallow.

CHAPTER FORTY-NINE

James and Sarah

Exhaustion had wrapped itself around her body, mind, and spirit. She felt defeated. Sitting in the dark, on the side of her bed, she only wanted to crawl under the covers and forget the day, but she willed herself up. The bedroom curtains billowed in a soft breeze. The tree limbs danced in the wind. Gathering energy, she walked across the room and stood looking out the open window into the darkness of the night. She let tears spill from her eyes in the darkness of her room and the night. Her tears were a cathartic release.

In the distance, thunder rumbled. A gentle breeze caressed her face, drying the tears. Returning to her bed, she began to undress, shedding her clothes like the day's burdens of helplessness and disappointment. Stepping out of the discarded garments, she donned a nightshirt and stretched out on her bed, yearning for sleep to envelop her. As slumber beckoned, a sudden noise jolted her awake. Sitting up, she noticed the rain and assumed the sound was thunder. But as she settled back, the noise came again. It wasn't thunder; someone was knocking at her door. Glancing at the clock, which read eleven forty-five, she wondered aloud, "Who could it be?" Reluctantly, she left her bed, retrieved her bathrobe, and fumbled with the sleeves. After putting on her robe, she turned on the stairway light, gripped the banister, and descended. Who would brave the storm to knock at her door? Could Donald have reconsidered? As she reached the final step, another knock sounded. "Who's there?" Sarah called.

"Me!" A voice called back. "It's me, James."

A massive lightning bolt streaked across the sky when she opened the door. James stood in the doorway, raindrops cascading down his face from his soaked hair. Sarah grasped his arm and pulled him into the safety of the house. "Come in! What are you doing here?" A clap of thunder vibrated the house as she closed the door, and the lights went out. "Damn! Don't move. Let me get a flashlight."

James could sense the rainwater trickling down his body, pooling at his feet. He embraced the obscurity of the night. His head pounded, his heart thrummed rapidly, and his stomach twisted into knots. He was at a loss for words, uncertain how to say what he had come to tell her.

Sarah returned holding a flashlight waist level. "You are soaking wet. You need to get out of those wet clothes."

"I'll be alright."

She moved the flashlight's beam to his face, "Don't be silly."

"Seriously, Sarah, I'll be alright."

"Whatever you say. I don't want you sitting on my sofa, so let's go into the kitchen."

A Mother's White Lie

He followed her into the kitchen. James felt like he was walking the last mile. She pulled out a chair from the kitchen table. "Have a seat." She walked over to a cabinet, opened a drawer, and removed a candle and matches. She lit the candle and placed it in an empty wine bottle she had planned to discard after drinking the last bit from the bottle following her return from Greener Pastures. After placing the bottle in front of James, she said, "I'm going to get some towels from the bathroom."

After she left the room, he pushed the bottle to the side. He didn't want his face illuminated by the candle flame. When he talked to her, he didn't want to see her face, and he didn't want her to see his. He wiped water dripping down his face from his hair with his hand.

Sarah returned to the kitchen, threw a towel to James, and moved towards the cupboard to search for another candle. "Why are you here? James, is there something wrong?"

James covered his head and face with the towel. "I was wondering how things went with Donald."

She stood still in the darkness. Puzzled she asked, "You came out in this storm because you were wondering how things went with Donald? Are you for real?"

James sat holding the towel to his face. Sarah stood leaning against the sink peering at James through the light from the candle. "James, what's going on? I know you didn't come out in this storm to see how things went with Donald. You could've called me to ask me that."

James lifted his face from the towel. He could feel a lump in his throat. He swallowed hard. "Sarah, I need to tell you something."

Sarah started to move toward the table.

He could see her silhouette moving towards him. "Stop! Please don't sit here with me. Go back to where you were."

Sarah froze. "James, what's wrong? You are scaring me."

"Please forgive me."

Sarah was feeling confused and scared. She could not understand why James was there asking her to forgive him. "Forgive you for what? James, what have you done?"

"You're going to hate me."

"James, you're like a brother to me. I could never hate you."

As James lowered his head, the lights came on. Sarah could now see James's trembling hands holding the towel.

"James, you're trembling. What's wrong?"

James took another deep breath and slowly released it. "Sarah, sit down."

Puzzled, she searched his face for some clue of what was wrong. "But you just told me…."

Not looking at her, "I know. I know what I just said. Please sit down."

"James, you sound upset … angry. What is it?"

He was angry at Robert for asking him to do what he had made him promise not to do. He remembered Robert specifically saying *I'll come home on my own time. When I decide the time, I want to be the one to tell Sarah why I left.*

Fear began to seize her heart and mind. She had never witnessed James in such a state. The thought of what he might disclose was unimaginable to her. She approached the table, pulled out a chair, and gently seated herself. James remained with his head down. Sarah reached out to place her hands over his, but he withdrew his hands from hers. Abruptly pushing back from the table, he stood up and strode to the sink where Sarah had previously been. Confounded by his actions, she turned her gaze towards him.

"Sarah, this will be easier if you don't look at me."

"Okay. Whatever you say." Sarah sat erect in the chair, looking at the white kitchen wall.

"Sarah…."

"Yes."

"Do you remember when I went to the football game in Baltimore?"

"Yes. That was a long time ago."

"Well, I didn't share everything that happened on that trip with you."

"James, it's alright. You don't have to share everything with me."

"Sarah, I just need you to be quiet and listen."

Sarah nodded her head, acknowledging she understood.

"Remember I told you about a little jazz club I went to?"

Sarah nodded her head.

"I didn't tell you when I was at the club, Robert came in."

Sarah's body tensed, motionless, her gaze fixed on the wall ahead. The fact that he had seen Robert and hadn't told her left her uncertain of her emotions.

"We talked, and I met him the next day. The rumor we heard about him is true. He is now going by the name Richard Fallon. He told me it was all Rose's idea."

Sarah couldn't believe what she was hearing. She started to turn around.

"No, please let me finish. He made me swear I would keep his secret."

Sarah's anger surged from deep within her. Her heart seemed ready to burst from her chest. Unable to sit and stare at the blank kitchen wall any longer, she shoved her chair back from the table. Tears cascaded down her cheeks as she murmured, "You knew his whereabouts when I spoke of hiring a detective to locate him. Twenty-seven years! Twenty-seven damn years! If you vowed to guard his secret, why reveal it to me now?"

James had never witnessed Sarah this angry. He had braced for tears and shouting, but her whispers unsettled him, even more than his dread of confessing about Robert. Now, as she faced him, he wanted to disappear. He found himself instinctively pushing his lower back against the sink. Clearing his throat, he managed to say, "Robert is here."

"What do you mean here?"

"Charlie's father contacted Robert when he was a senior in high school. They kept in touch. When Charlie's parents died, they left all their properties to Robert. He said he came home to be close to Rose. While staying in your father's parents' home, he fell and broke his hip. When he was told that he would need to go to a rehabilitation center for a while, he requested to be placed at Greener Pastures."

"What? How long has he been here?"

"Almost three months."

"Why Greener Pastures?"

"Because he knew Rose was there."

"How?"

"He said he has been writing to her since he left home. Sarah, he needs to be the one to tell his story."

Sarah was in disbelief at the revelation. She understood that her twin brother had harbored secrets before he decided to leave home and reinvent himself. Her heart started pounding, her legs turned to jelly, and a wave of nausea swept over her. Grasping for support, she found a chair behind her. "This is preposterous! You are telling me Robert has been in Lynchburg for three months and is at Greener Pastures…and Mom knew where he was all this time?"

"Yes." James stepped toward her. "Are you alright?"

She was speechless, sinking slowly into the chair. James retrieved a glass from the cabinet over the sink, filled it with water, and offered it to her. Her hands shook as she reached for the glass. She brought it to her lips and sipped cautiously. With her voice returning, she inquired, "How long has he been there?"

"I am not sure exactly, but several weeks."

"Is there anything more you need to tell me?"

James was eager to depart. He transitioned from the sink to the kitchen door, which opened into the hallway, leading to the front door. James leaned against the kitchen door frame for support before speaking. He coughed to clear his throat and noted, "Robert witnessed your discussion with Donald yesterday. He was seated in the hallway, just outside the community room."

"What? He was where?" Her anger had given way to numbness. "James, why are you telling me this now?"

"Robert called and asked me to," James said, apologizing. He began to walk out of the kitchen, eager to leave. He paused but didn't look back. "I'm sorry," he repeated. Then he departed, gently closing the door behind him.

CHAPTER FIFTY

Sarah

Throughout the night, Sarah's gaze was fixed on the shadows flickering across her bedroom wall. The confrontations with Donald and James consumed her thoughts. Donald had denied Sidney the chance to see Rose, leaving Sarah powerless to prevent her mother's swift decline into despair. Her twin brother had chosen to live as a white man, boldly claiming to James that their mother Rose had encouraged him to renounce his family and his identity. James had revealed that Robert, the brother she once cherished, had kept secrets from her before his departure. Sleep remained elusive. Dawn's early light began to seep through her window. Glancing at the clock, it read seven forty-five. Despite her desire to hide away beneath her blankets, duties called. With a sense of resolve, she rose from her bed and reached for her bathrobe at its foot.

Sarah resolved not to visit Greener Pastures that day, confident her mother wouldn't notice her absence. She phoned the director to detail the circumstances. Mrs. Jefferson, the director, was taken aback upon discovering that Rose's son was undergoing rehabilitation at Greener Pastures. She consented to book a conference room for Sarah and Rose's meeting with Robert. Sarah inquired if Mrs. Jefferson could notify Robert about the meeting's scheduled time and location.

She needed a strong cup of black coffee. Leaving her room, she halted at Robert's door. Instinctively, her hand reached for the knob—this was her refuge for problems and closeness to her twin. But her hand froze mid-reach. She balled it into a fist, pounding on the door as tears streamed down her cheeks. "Damn you! Damn you! Damn you!" she shouted, pressing her forehead against the door, hearing Robert's laughter and their shared secrets. Turning away, she descended the stairs and, halfway down the stairs, she screamed.

A Mother's White Lie

CHAPTER FIFTY-ONE

Richard

He had expected Sarah to come bursting through the doors of Greener Pastures last night, but she didn't. He had braced for her rage, yet it never arrived. Perhaps James hadn't followed through with his request. The agony of silence was excruciating, but he preferred it to the tsunami of wrath and judgment he anticipated from Sarah. How he would respond remained uncertain. He spent the first part of the night awake, mentally rehearsing potential conversations with Sarah and his possible replies. None of the scenarios ended well.

He longed for sleep, yet it escaped him as the day he departed from home replayed in his mind like a persistent film. *I remember a soft knock on my bedroom door the night before I left. I walked across the room to the door. I stood there with my hand on the* doorknob. I knew it was Mom. She softly whispered my name, "Robert." I opened the door. We stood staring at one another. I could see the sadness in her eyes. She looked past me. "Are you packed?"

"Yes, but...."

She softly placed her hands on my lips. "I'll have breakfast ready for you at five o'clock."

"But Mom...."

"You get some rest now. I'll see you at breakfast. Don't forget to say your prayers."

"Live my life as a white man? Mom, I'm not sure about this."

"Robert, God gave you an advantage He didn't give your sister."

"How will Sarah feel about me doing that?"

"She must never know. It won't be easy because your family will no longer be a part of your life."

"Mom, I can't...."

"Robert, you must!"

"But I will be living a lie!"

"Robert, get some rest."

I tried to sleep, but I couldn't. I could only think my life would soon become a lie.

When morning light drifted through my window, I heard Mom going downstairs to the kitchen. I heard birds singing outside my window, but their song was melancholy. Did the birds know what I was about to do? I reluctantly got out of my bed for the last time as a Black man. I dressed, grabbed my two suitcases, and quietly went downstairs to the kitchen. Mom was standing at the back door. She turned around when she heard me. She looked at me. Her eyes were sad. She held out her hand. I took it in mine. She *said, "That pear tree…." Tears streamed down her face. I knew the pear tree was where Mom and Dad professed their love. We sat at the table not saying one word. After eating breakfast, she hugged me so tight. I wondered what she was thinking, but we said nothing. She handed me a one-way Greyhound Bus ticket. Tears ran down my face as I walked down Fifth Street with my suitcases. When I got on the bus, I sat behind the bus driver.*

The sound of the toilet flushing jolted Richard back into the present. He had not heard his roommate get out of bed.

CHAPTER FIFTY-TWO

Greener Pastures

Richard resolved to strip away the veils of his existence: the lies, fear, guilt, and silence. As he walked into the community room, the television blared news of a Northeast blackout impacting New York and parts of New Jersey. Lillie chanted her usual sales pitch for cigars, cigarettes, and Tiparillos. Meanwhile, Brittney and Janie Ruth sat at a table with Bessie, who was deeply absorbed in solving a word search puzzle.

Janie Ruth saw Richard and gestured to him to join them.

Richard scanned the room for Rose before slowly walking over to where Janie Ruth and the other women were gathered.

Janie Ruth motioned to an empty chair, "Sit down and take a load off."

Richard smiled, "Thank you." He pulled out a chair, "Good morning, ladies."

Brittney and Bessie mumbled good morning.

Richard lowered himself in the chair and looked at Janie Ruth, "How is your roommate doing?"

Janie Ruth shook her head and said, "I feel so sorry for her."

Pretending not to know what Janie meant, Richard asked, "What do you mean?"

Janie Ruth and Brittney stared at Richard in disbelief. Brittney asked, "Didn't you hear what happened yesterday in this room?"

Before Richard could reply, Bessie sprang up like a jack-in-the-box, launching into a tirade. "Sarah was begging Donald to allow his father to visit Rose. Meanwhile, Rose was shouting for Sidney, though she kept calling him Charlie. Donald stormed out, and Sarah chased after him. All the while, poor Rose sat here, unaware of the unfolding drama, until she stood and screamed, 'C-H-A-R-L-I-E!'"

Janie Ruth lowered her head. All eyes were on Bessie. With slow and deliberate enunciation, Janie Ruth said, "Bessie, be quiet!"

Bessie looked at Janie Ruth, not understanding why she was telling her to be quiet. "Brittney just asked him if he knew what happened here. I'm just filling him in."

Brittney chimed in, "Bessie, you're just a show-off. You want to show that your short-term memory is still working."

Bessie laughed, "What's wrong with that? I don't do these word searches for nothing."

Still sitting in her chair, Brittney put her hands on her hips, "I might not remember what day it is, but I can remember the breakfast egg menu, so there, Miss Depends."

Bessie retorted, "You can kiss my Depends!"

While Janie Ruth and Richard stared at one another in disbelief, Emily approached the table. She asked, "Is tonight bingo night?"

Brittney yelled, "No! Go sit down somewhere."

Emily asked, "What did you say?"

Brittney and Bessie yelled in unison, "Sit down!"

Janie Ruth looked from Emily to Richard, "Can you believe this?"

Emily asked, "Who conceived?"

While Bessie yelled at Emily about her hearing aid, Richard leaned over to Janie Ruth and whispered, "I need to talk with you. Can we go somewhere private?"

Janie Ruth responded with a confirming nod. Together, they pushed back their chairs and left the community room.

CHAPTER FIFTY-THREE

Janie Ruth and Richard

Is confession good for the soul? He needed to talk with someone before seeing Sarah, so Richard decided to confide in Janie Ruth. After all, Janie Ruth was Rose's roommate and Richard's friend.

Janie Ruth guided Richard to the deserted courtyard. A cobblestone path led to stone benches positioned around a grand water fountain. Red and yellow roses had been planted strategically around the courtyard. Janie Ruth led Richard to one of the benches facing the fountain; they sat without speaking.

After a few awkward minutes of silence, Janie Ruth asked, "How are things going? Will you be going home soon?"

A Mother's White Lie

Janie Ruth's inquiries seemed to ease Richard's tension. He inhaled deeply and said, "I'm doing alright. Physical therapy has become quite challenging. I've been ascending stairs to enhance my range of motion and fortify my hip. I'm looking forward to leaving earlier rather than later."

"I'm happy for you." Janie Ruth could sense Richard didn't want to talk about his physical therapy. She was curious but didn't want to ask him why he wanted to speak with her. She liked Richard and knew she would miss him when he left.

Richard turned slightly so he would be able to see Janie Ruth's face. Then he said, "Janie Ruth."

"Yes."

He dabbed his face with a handkerchief pulled from his pocket. "I... I need to tell you something, but before I do, I need your promise not to judge me."

Janie Ruth found it unimaginable that this white man would request her not to judge him. She turned to Richard, smiled, and said, "Who am I to judge anyone?"

Richard chuckled nervously. "You say that now. I have only told one other person what I'm about to tell you."

"Who was that?"

"My uncle. I told him because I had no choice."

"Why do you want to tell me?"

Richard lowered his head. Breathing deeply, he raised his gaze to meet Janie Ruth's eyes and whispered, "Rose is my mother."

Richard and Janie Ruth locked gazes. He attempted to decipher her expression, but it was impassive. He wondered if she had not heard or grasped his words. Awaiting her reply, he watched as Janie Ruth remained motionless. Time stretched on, and then, wordlessly, Janie Ruth leaned in toward Richard, her search for his blackness evident. Shaking her head in disbelief, she spoke, "I've heard of people doing this."

"I look like my father. He was white. Sarah is my twin sister."

Janie Ruth's mouth fell open in astonishment. "Wow!" She scrutinized his face with disbelief, seeking any slight resemblance to Rose. At last, Janie Ruth inquired, "Why haven't you mentioned this until now? Why haven't you spent time with Rose?"

"I knew she wouldn't know who I was. When I was told I needed rehab, I saw it as a blessing. I could see my mother every day. I had no idea about the Sidney situation."

"So, you know about what happened last night?"

"Yes, I was sitting in the hallway last night, but Sarah didn't notice me."

"How long have you been passing?"

"Since I graduated high school. Passing was my mother's idea."

Looking at him confused, "Rose wanted you to live your life as a white man?"

"Yes. She said she wanted me to have the best that life had to offer. She made me promise not to tell Sarah. My father left all his properties to my mother. Mom said she would make sure Sarah had the best life had to offer her as an African American female. I love my mother. I was being an obedient son. I understood what she told me to do hurt her to the core of her soul. I also know her love for me allowed her to bear that pain."

Astounded by his response, Janie Ruth sat silent for a moment. Shaking her head in disbelief, she said, "I have heard of people doing this, but I have never met one who did it. What is it like living on the other side?"

"There was always the fear of being found out. I couldn't be with my family and friends. I spent a lot of time alone, especially on holidays. But passing for white has its privileges because when white men looked at me, they saw themselves. I've gotten job interviews, smiles, and welcomes I wouldn't have gotten if they knew my secret. White women don't feel threatened and cross to the other side of the street when they see me coming towards them; store owners don't follow me in their stores; police don't look at me as a suspect; white people don't wipe their hands after shaking mine; racists are very comfortable making racist jokes around me."

Still shaking her head, Janie Ruth blurred, "My grandma used to say you can put the truth in a river five days after a lie and the truth will always catch up to the lie. Your life has been one big lie." Janie Ruth felt regret as soon as the words left her lips. "I'm sorry. I shouldn't have said that."

"No need to apologize for the truth."

"This may sound like a stupid question, but I have to ask, are you happy living as a white man?"

"It's not a stupid question. I've spent most of my life trying to avoid the real me. I'm seventy-one years old and I don't know if I truly know what happiness is."

"I'm sorry."

"What are you sorry about?

"Life is too short for you not to know happiness."

"I understand that now. I sacrificed my family for things I couldn't attain while being true to myself."

"Richard...."

"Robert ... my name is Robert."

Janie Ruth felt a surge of anger welling up within her, the cause of which eluded her. Without remorse, she snapped, "You could have been a Black journalist. Rose may have proposed that you live as a white man, but the decision was yours to make."

The abrupt shift in Janie Ruth's tone made Robert feel uneasy. "I know."

"Richard ... I mean Robert, why are you telling me this?"

"Because you share a room with my mother and because I consider you a friend."

The pain in his eyes was evident, and she had no desire to deepen his anguish. "As I mentioned, who am I to judge? You're right, you do need a friend right now and I will not turn my back on you," she asserted. Janie Ruth observed him silently, uncertain of how to offer solace. His appearance was that of someone adrift. "Would a hug help, my friend?" she offered

Robert nodded yes.

Janie Ruth wrapped her arms around him, and tears escaped his eyes.

CHAPTER FIFTY-FOUR

Sarah

Trapped inside the crevices of her mind. She was having a mental meltdown. What if what James had told her held any truth? She would be forced to accept the realization her mother's prevarication had manipulated realities.

At ten-thirty in the morning, Sarah hadn't reached the kitchen yet. Instead, she was huddled in a corner at the bottom of the stairs. She had thought a day to herself would bring calm, but it only deepened her wallowing in emotion. Confusion over what to feel overwhelmed her. Anger, pain, and a sense of betrayal consumed her. If James's revelations were true, then her mother had lied to her. She had believed her mother rushed to meet the mailman, hoping for news from Robert. But, according to James, her mother was eager to check the mail because she was in contact with Robert and wanted to keep it from her. She had assumed her mother's silence about Robert stemmed from pain, yet if James was correct, her mother hadn't experienced the agony she felt when Robert departed. She had sacrificed her happiness to care for a mother who had been deceitful. Haunting questions echoed in her mind: "Was I merely her servant, her caretaker because I was the Black child? Did she ever love me?" These thoughts triggered an acute, piercing pain in her head and heart, making her feel nauseous. Overcome by her emotions, Sarah began to weep uncontrollably.

CHAPTER FIFTY-FIVE

Sarah and Robert

She hadn't slept. As the morning sunlight filtered through her bedroom window, Sarah lay in bed staring at the ceiling. With a sigh, she cast aside the covers and pulled herself out of the bed. She slid her feet into her slippers and reluctantly went to the bathroom to get herself ready. She leaned into the mirror to take a closer look at her face. Her eyes were puffy and bloodshot. She took a shower and put on a khaki skirt with a soft green sleeveless blouse.

She pulled a London Fog raincoat off a hanger in her closet. She checked the time and descended the stairs. She stopped at the bottom of the stairs and stared at the corner she had crouched in the last evening.

The weather is perfect, she thought. Dreary and angry. Large raindrops, pregnant with her pain, smashed angrily against the windshield of her car. Her windshield wipers desperately pushed the pregnant raindrops away. She found a parking space in front of the building.

As a nurse's aide wheeled Rose into the conference room, Sarah arrived simultaneously. She offered a smile and her thanks. Pausing, Sarah looked at Rose, pondering the stranger she called Mom. She maneuvered her mother's wheelchair inside the room. After draping her raincoat over a chair, Sarah focused on her mother. Rose seemed more lucid than she had been since Sidney's departure. Sarah leaned in to peck her mother's cheek with a kiss. In response, Rose tenderly stroked her daughter's face. Holding her mother's hands, Sarah gently withdrew, her eyes brimming with tears.

Sarah whispered, "I love you, Mom." The look on Rose's face made Sarah feel her mother knew who she was. Just as Sarah was about to ask her mother if she recognized her, there was a soft knock on the door. Sarah retreated behind her mother's wheelchair. Robert slowly turned the doorknob. He entered the room and quietly closed the door. Dressed in the same khakis and green Brooks Brothers shirt he wore on his first day at Greener Pastures, he stood facing his mother and sister. He clutched a large brown envelope in his left hand. They stood in an awkward silence that seemed to stretch into eternity. Just as Robert was about to break the silence, Sarah blurted out angrily, "So, the dead have arisen."

"Hello to you too, Sarah." Robert was not sure how he should respond. He didn't want to argue, but he knew there was no avoiding it.

Sarah stepped from behind Rose's wheelchair. She looked at her brother from head to toe.

"Look at you – Mr. White Man!"

"Sarah, we both lived as we were born." After the words tumbled from his lips, he knew they would only provoke her.

"No! I have lived true to my birth," she declared. Rose adjusted herself in her wheelchair. Sarah bent down to ensure she was okay. Once she confirmed Rose was fine, she gradually stood up straight. She met Robert's gaze, bit her lower lip, and shook her head. Through clenched teeth, she affirmed, "I was born Black, and I have lived that way."

Robert strode to the conference table, laid the envelope upon it, and rested his hands on the back of a chair at the table's end. "I was born white," he declared, "and that's how I've lived my life."

Sarah looked at Robert with disdain, "What are you talking about? We're twins! We share the same mother, and she isn't white."

"And we both had the same father, and he was white."

"So, what?"

Robert chuckled.

"So, you find this funny."

"No." Robert gave her a sarcastic grin. "So, you believe one drop of Black blood makes you Black. Don't you think it's interesting that society has determined that a white woman can have a Black baby, but a Black woman can't have a white baby? Mom had a white baby, and she had a black baby."

"You're just trying to justify turning your back on your family. And you dare to smile about it."

Shaking his head in disagreement, "I didn't turn my back on my family."

"Well, what would you call it?"

He pulled the chair from under the table. "Do you mind if I sit down? I can't stand too long without having some discomfort."

"Why should it matter to you whether I mind? What I felt or thought when you left home didn't matter to you."

Robert pulled the chair back from the table. He slowly lowered himself into it. He touched the envelope which was directly in front of him. Then he gently pushed it to the side.

Sarah and Rose were seated at the opposite end of the table. Even though Rose seemed oblivious to what was happening, Sarah maneuvered her mother's wheelchair, positioning it to face Robert's end of the table. She wanted Robert to confront their mother if he dared to place the blame on her for his actions. Standing behind their mother, Sarah fixed a steely gaze on her brother, as if ready to launch an attack. "Why did you leave the way you did? You just left a note. You could have had the decency to tell me to my face."

"I did what our mom instructed me to do."

With her hands gripping the push handles of the wheelchair, Sarah looked down at Rose. "Don't lie on Mom."

"I'm not lying."

"Robert, look at her! Why would she tell you to do something like that?"

"You remember during my senior year I had a job cleaning offices in the Allied Arts Building?"

"Yes, I remember. What does that have to do with anything? Your leaving hurt Mom. Mom's heart never forgot you."

"And my heart never forgot her or you."

Robert's words pierced her heart. She tried to control her emotions. Although she fought the tears in her eyes, they could be heard in her voice. "Then why did you do it?"

Robert could feel his sister hurting. He wanted to embrace her. He wished he could go back in time and change everything, but he couldn't, so he continued trying to explain. "Sarah." He needed to say her name. He did not want to fight with her. "That was what I was trying to explain to you. One day after work, I changed my clothes and waited for the bus. When I got on the bus, there weren't any empty seats. The bus driver made an old Black man get up and give me his seat. He thought I was white. It bothered me, but I took the seat. When I got home, I told Mom what happened on the bus. I remember her words like it was yesterday. She said, 'You're going to graduate from high school. You're going to leave Virginia, and you're going to go to New York and live as a white man.' Sarah, I didn't want to leave my friends and my family, but Mom said it was the best thing for me. She told me the best gift she could give me was to let me go to live my life as society saw me – a white man. She told me that would be the only way I'd have the best chances in life."

"Mom would've never said something like that to you."

"But she did. Sarah, I wrote to Mom every month, and she wrote to me." Robert pulled a letter from the brown envelope and began to read.

Dear Son,

I didn't expect to hear from you so soon. I would've loved to have kept you here with me. If I could've made this a perfect world for you, I would have. My heart wants all the best things in life for you. Know that God makes no mistakes. You're who you are for a reason. I hope you will love yourself enough that you will find ways to fill those lonely times when you're missing family. I love you enough to let you go to find a career and happiness that I know you wouldn't have been able to find if you'd stayed here.

The day I gave birth to you was one of the happiest moments of my life. You're my first baby and without loving your sister any less, you'll always be special to me. Every mother wants her children to do well. Every mother wants her children to have chances at life she didn't have. Every mother wants to hold her children, her babies, close to her breasts. The day you left, I knew I'd probably never see you again, but I was okay with that because I felt in my heart you were going to have a good life.

Take care of yourself and remember to always look to God. Stay in prayer and you'll be fine.

Thank you so much for the money.

Love you with all my heart.

Mom

"I don't believe Mom wrote that. Let me see it."

Robert pushed himself away from the table. He walked down to the other end of the table and placed the letter in front of Sarah. She examined it.

"It looks like her handwriting."

"Sarah, it's her handwriting."

She retorted sharply, "So, you're our mother's white lie!"

Robert winced. The words struck a chord. He realized he had been living a falsehood, but when it came to his mother and their relationship, he had never seen himself as her little white lie.

A Mother's White Lie

CHAPTER FIFTY-SIX

Sarah and Robert

Trying to rid himself of the pain of his sister's words, he exhaled and spoke. "She was scared, Sarah."

Trying to control the anger she felt bubbling in the pit of her stomach like a volcano waiting to erupt, she asked, "Scared of what? Being caught in the lie, the two of you concocted?"

Robert knew a verbal response would cause the release of the explosive anger he could feel rumbling in his sister. Without saying a word, he pulled another letter from the envelope. He rose from his chair and walked back to his sister's end of the table. He laid the letter on the table in front of her.

Sarah's eyes were fixed on the letter. Robert returned to his seat at the end of the table with measured steps. Pausing, he glanced at his sister; her attention remained on the letter. Gradually, Sarah's eyes moved from the letter to their mother. Rose was sitting, her head bowed. A surge of anger welled up in Sarah. *How could she profess love yet lie to me for so long?* She pondered whether Rose grasped the gravity of the situation. Shifting her attention back, Sarah lifted the letter and silently read it.

Dear Son,

How are you doing? How is your job? It has been six months since Sarah went with me to see the doctor. I am scared. Last week I couldn't find my way home. I was on Church Street. I had no idea how to get home. Some man was driving by and asked me if I wanted a ride home. I asked him if he knew where I lived. He laughed and said yes. He brought me home. I don't know who he was. I didn't tell Sarah. I don't want to upset her. She worries about me. Did I tell you she was seeing someone? I haven't met him. She hasn't mentioned him lately. I told her when it is time, take me to Greener

Pastures. I can't remember if I told you that. I'm not ready to go to Greener Pastures yet. I'm so scared. I am not sleeping at night. Soon I won't know Sarah. How can I forget my child? How can I live a life and forget it? I won't remember anything. I got to go. If I remember, I will write more next time.

Love you with all my heart.

Mom

After finishing the letter, Sarah was too bewildered and furious to lay it down. She was oblivious to Rose, who leaned in and, with a frail arm, snatched the letter from her grasp. Witnessing this, Robert sprang up and hastened to the opposite end of the table where his sister sat.

Startled by Rose's abrupt action, Sarah recoiled, tearing the letter. "Mom, what are you doing? Give it back to me!"

"No, it's mine."

Robert's attention shifted between Sarah and Rose. This was a different Rose than who he had seen since he had been at Greener Pastures. She seemed to be suddenly infused with a surge of awareness. Sarah, equally surprised, leaned in and gently extracted the torn letter from her mother's grasp.

Rose's grip on the letter weakened as her surge of energy faded. Turning to Robert, she remarked, "She is so mean."

Robert smiled at Rose, "It's alright. She's not trying to be mean. She's upset with me."

Rose glared at Sarah while speaking to Robert, "Don't let her be mean to you."

Perplexed yet mildly entertained by Rose's unexpected display of boldness, Robert grinned and said, "I won't."

Rose's frail hands swept over her lap, smoothing out her dress. She leaned forward, peering intently. "Robert, is that you?"

Stunned, Robert stooped over in front of her, "Yes, Mom, it's me."

Sarah placed the letter on the table. "Mom?" There was life in Rose's eyes. Sarah reached out and took her mom's hand in her own. "Mom, do you know who I am?"

Rose said nothing. She pulled her hands from Sarah's hands. The room was quiet. Rose sat staring at Robert.

Robert reached for Rose's hand, "Mom, how are you feeling?"

Rose smiled. "Robert, are you going to work tonight? You know you need to clean those lawyers' offices."

"No, I'm not working tonight. I want to spend some time with you, Mom."

Sarah felt like her heart was breaking into a thousand pieces. Her mother seemed to recognize Robert but not her. She was the one who had given up a chance at happiness for her. The anger she had been directing at her twin brother was now turning to her mother. Sarcastically, "Mom, Robert doesn't clean offices anymore." She turned to Robert, "Tell us Robert, what do you do now?"

Robert rubbed his brow, trying to prevent the headache he felt coming. He understood Sarah's anger, and he could see the hurt in her eyes. He sighed, stood up, and said, "I'm a journalist."

Rose said nothing. Sarah wanted to scream. She was haunted with the thought of whether her mother ever loved her as much as she loved Robert. The letter she read said nothing about Rose telling Robert to pass for white. She was ready to lash out, but her emotions were strangling her. Words stuck in her throat. In her heart, she knew Robert had to be lying. She swallowed hard. It felt like the lump in her throat was taking up occupancy in her chest. It felt like she had been stabbed, and someone was twisting the knife. With enormous contempt and anger, she asked. "When did you become a journalist, Robert?"

Robert felt a sudden shift in Sarah's tone. He decided to keep his emotions in check. "Sarah, when I went to New York, I got a job in the mailroom of a newspaper. I went to school at night, and I worked my way out of the mailroom."

Rose's feeble arms trembled as she pushed against her wheelchair to reposition herself. Rose turned to Sarah. "Sarah, what are you talking about? You and your brother are still in high school."

Sarah's lower jaw dropped hearing Rose address her by name. "Mom, you know me."

"Of course, I know you. Where did that mean lady go?"

Before Sarah could respond, Robert interjected, "She has gone. Hasn't she, Sarah?" He hoped his response would cause Sarah to be a bit more amicable.

Sarah rolled her eyes at Robert. She reached for Rose's hand and gently rubbed it. "Mom, Robert isn't in high school, and according to him, you told him to go to New York and pass for white."

Rose tilted her head to one side. "Sarah, what's wrong with you?"

"Mom, Robert is lying on you."

"Sarah, why are you saying your brother is lying?"

"Mom, Robert said you told him to pass for white."

"Sarah, that is ridiculous. I've told you both you shouldn't fight with one another. Now, Sarah, get up."

Sarah didn't know what to do. She sat staring at her mother.

"Go ahead and do as I say!"

Sarah felt like a little girl being scolded by her mother. She placed her hands flat on the table for leverage. She slowly rose from her chair.

Rose looked up at her son. "Robert, I want you and Sarah to hug one another. Go ahead."

Robert moved slowly towards his sister. He extended open arms. Sarah stood staring at him. She had a churning feeling in the pit of her stomach. She wanted to do as her mother requested but couldn't make herself walk into her brother's arms.

Rose raised her arms. Her hands trembled as she directed Sarah to move toward her brother. "Go ahead, Sarah! I'm not going to always be here for you. As you get older, I've told the both of you that you'll only have each other, so you must always love each other."

Sarah stepped into Robert's embrace with hesitation. The comfort she had craved since his departure was finally within reach, yet she couldn't permit herself to stay in his arms for long. Gently, she pulled away. Turning to her mother, she caught what seemed to be a smile spreading across her face. Sarah settled back into her chair and, picking up the letter from the table, said, "Mom, Robert mentioned you wrote this."

Rose took the letter from Sarah. She flipped it over. "What is this?"

Sarah looked from Robert to Rose. "A letter Robert said you wrote to him."

Rose continued to flip the letter over and over in her hands. Rose sat for a moment staring at it. Then she placed the letter on her head.

The light had faded from Rose's eyes. Sarah felt her heart thumping in her chest. Her mother was again lost to her, withdrawn into a realm of shadows. Struggling to restrain her tears, Sarah whispered, "No, Mom, it's not a hat." She extended her hand to take the letter, but Rose clung to it firmly.

Robert, like Sarah, understood that their mother had descended into a profound darkness, yet he felt gratitude. The final memory he had of his mother was when he was eighteen. She had recognized him before the lie. He stooped and extended his hand for the letter, and she handed it to him. He then passed it to Sarah. Rose looked at him and offered a smile. Perhaps she hadn't truly left them after all.

A period of silence had passed before anyone uttered a word, a silence that was a welcomed relief. Robert's hip began to ache, prompting him to stand. As he leaned on the arm of Rose's wheelchair for support, she extended her hands and tenderly stroked his face. "Charlie! Charlie, you've come to visit me," she exclaimed.

Sarah's frown deepened, a wave of nausea threatening to overwhelm her. Overcome with the day's events, she realized she had not thought about Donald and Sidney. With a grimace, she uttered, "Mom?"

Rose tilted her head to one side. She looked at Sarah and asked, "Who are you?"

A Mother's White Lie

With tears in her voice, Sarah replied, "I'm Sarah. I'm your daughter."

Rose glanced at Robert, offering a timid smile. She then shifted her attention to Sarah. "Could you please move over so Charlie can sit next to me?" she asked.

Sarah shook her head, exasperated. "Mom, he's not Charlie! He's your son, and I'm your daughter."

Robert pleaded, "Sarah, please let her have this moment. Let her believe I'm our father if she wants to believe it. No one is being hurt."

Sarah stood up slowly from the chair. "You would think that way! Lies are painful! I never lie to her."

Robert walked behind Rose's wheelchair before taking the seat that Sarah had just left. "Sarah, I know you're upset with me," he said. "But this moment isn't about us—it's about our mother. Let's give her this moment of happiness."

Rose extended her hand to touch Robert's arm as she spoke, "I've been waiting for you."

Robert gently kissed her on the forehead. "I'm so sorry it has taken me so long to get back to see you."

Rose patted his hand. "You're here. You're here." Rose gently laid her head on his shoulder.

Sarah was overwhelmed with many emotions, unable to distinguish one from another. Her voice trembling, she said, "Robert, this is sick."

"Why? Mom deserves to be happy."

"Stop with this masquerade! Sidney is not Charlie, and you are not Charlie! Lying is not something I condone. You wouldn't know anything about that, would you?"

Robert sat silently for a moment. "You're just what Mom said – mean! Donald won't let Sidney come to visit her. What's the harm in her believing that I'm our father? Let her be happy for this moment! Mom knew she was dealing with Alzheimer's, and it scared her. I think it's great she has someone she loves. Love has a power that breaks through the darkness of Alzheimer's. The mind might not remember how to remember but love doesn't have to remember. When you build no walls around the heart, love happens. Love overcomes the darkness. Let her have this bit of light. This bit of happiness. Mom didn't allow herself to love anyone after Daddy was killed."

Sarah moved away from the table, concealing her hurt. She paused momentarily, her back turned to Robert and Rose. Once she regained her composure, she proceeded to the table's far end. "Mom never talked with me about being scared."

Robert could feel Sarah's pain. "I know. Sarah, she loves you so much. She didn't want to worry or upset you."

Rose, annoyed, patted Robert's hand. "Why are you talking to her? You're here to see me."

Robert kissed Rose's head again to reassure her he was there for her. "Yes, I'm here to see you, the love of my life."

Rose managed to smile. "You're so sweet." She laid her head on Robert's chest.

Despite the unpleasant encounter with his sister, Robert felt grateful for the moments spent with his mother. He had resigned himself to believe that he would never hold her again. Yet, here she was, very much alive and had acknowledged him briefly. Now, resting her head on his shoulder, she seemed at peace. Robert tenderly brushed her hair from her face. "No, you're sweet and pretty like the flower whose name you carry. Let's sit here together for a little while so I can talk with this lady."

Rose lifted her head. She positioned herself so she could see Robert's face. "Okay, as long as she doesn't try to flirt with you. You know young girls nowadays are frisky."

Robert kissed Rose on her forehead as she again placed her head on his shoulder.

Sarah mumbled, "There is no chance of that." She decided she would try to have a civil conversation with her brother. "Robert, you said Mom deserves happiness. I am not trying to be ugly. I want to know, have you been happy with your life choices?"

Robert gestured to a chair, "Please come and sit at this end of the table."

Sarah made her way to the table's end where her mother and brother sat. Drawing out a chair, she eased herself down into it, positioning herself to face her mother and brother.

Robert examined his twin sister's expression intently. He parted his lips to speak, then paused, ensuring his words would reflect his true sentiments. He fidgeted with his ear, letting his hand glide down his face to rest on his chin, veiling his mouth slightly. "I guess it depends on how you would define happiness. If you measure happiness with having success, well-being, and prosperity, I have all those things. I can say I'm content with my life, but I can't say I'm happy. I haven't known happiness since I left home. What I don't have is freedom."

The hope for a civil conversation was lost. Sarah threw her head back, laughing uproariously. Her laughter jarred Rose. Robert gently patted his mother as if she were an infant. She sighed, resting her head again on his shoulder. In frustration, Sarah raised and lowered her hands. "You are kidding, aren't you? You don't have what? You're passing for white, and with that comes freedom."

Robert shook his head. "Freedom isn't just about skin color."

She struggled to suppress her sarcasm, yet words laced with attitude sprang forth. "Really? You could've fooled me," she retorted. "Do enlighten me, why do you lack freedom?"

"I want to answer that question for you, but I need you not to say anything until I finish."

"Yes, sir, master." She wished she hadn't responded the way she did, but she was hurt when she needed Robert and he was not there. He was a missing part of her.

Robert's voice cracked. "Sarah, I'm not your master. I'm your twin brother!"

Robert's tone prompted Sarah to scrutinize his expression. She perceived the pain etched on his face for the first time since their reunion. "I'm sorry," she said. "Please, tell me why you feel you lack freedom."

He swallowed hard before he spoke. "Truth is freedom."

"Yes, it is!"

"Please, Sarah. I need to be able to say what I'm about to say. I won't be able to if you interrupt."

"I promise I will not say another word."

"Having control over your reality and not having your reality imposed upon you is freedom. Freedom is not living in fear. My reality was imposed upon me, and I've been living my life in constant fear. Afraid someone would find out who I am. Sarah, I have been totally … *totally* alone. I have had no one. Mom thought passing for white would allow me to live without fear. It didn't. Fear governed my life. I have allowed myself to have relationships, but afraid to take them to the next level. What if I got a girl pregnant? My secret could have been uncovered. Am I happy? I can only answer that question by saying there is no happiness in being all alone and afraid."

"Your reality was your choice."

"You're right. I know ultimately, passing for white was my choice, but I was doing what our mother asked me to do. After Daddy died, I wanted to be the perfect son. I didn't realize the price I would be paying."

"You're enslaved by your lies."

"Yes, I was. Sarah, earlier, you called me our mother's white lie. That cut me deep in my soul, but you're right. I was living a white lie. I was alone. I was homesick, and I felt our mother was ashamed of me. As a child, I fell on my knees many nights, praying and asking God to make me brown. I wanted to be like you, Sarah, so kids on the playground would accept me the way they did you."

Wow! She thought. He had never shared this with her. It was at this moment she realized she had her own secret. "Robert, we were both teased. And when we got to high school, you were more accepted than I was. Especially by the girls."

"Yeah, but the scars were already there. I wanted them to stop calling me Whitey. I hated being teased. It hurt like hell when kids would say I wasn't your brother. They said things like my real parents must have hated me if they dropped me off in a black neighborhood. After I had been in New York for about a month, I felt like I wanted to end it all. I sat down and wrote Mom a letter. I asked her if she loved me. If she was ashamed of me. Why did she tell me to turn my back on my family? I brought her answer, to my letter, with me."

Rose had fallen asleep, her mouth slightly open. Robert didn't want to wake her, so he carefully shifted his body to the side. He pulled a folded piece of paper from the front pocket of his trousers and placed it on his knee. With his free hand, he unfolded the letter and looked at Sarah. "Would you like to read it?" he asked.

"No, you read it."

Robert nodded his head. He wet his lips and began reading.

Dear Son,

My heart broke when I read your last letter. How can you doubt my love for you?

I love you so much. You and your sister are my heart. You are my life.

I want you and your sister to have a successful life. I feel Sarah will be alright. Your father made sure I didn't have to worry about anything. So, I will make sure she has every opportunity possible.

As for you, the life of a colored man is not an easy one. Life for colored men is dangerous. Colored men disappear. It's a terror I didn't want for you. Sometimes it's not safe for white men who associate with colored people. Before giving birth to you and your sister, I had no idea I could love anyone as much as I love you and your sister. I love you so much, I am willing to sacrifice my happiness and my wants for your happiness and success. I love you so much, I am willing to give my life for your security and happiness. Robert, I would prefer to have you at home so I can see you every day. So, I can hug you and hear your voice. But having you home, I would worry about your safety and happiness. Do you remember how you would cry about the way you were treated on the playground? I don't want you crying because of something you have no control over. I don't know why God made one of my twins to look like me and the other to look like your father. I feel God had His reason. I don't know if we will ever know the reason. Son, never doubt my love for you. Know I want you to have the best life has to offer. This was the only way I could see you getting it.

Robert, I love you with all my heart.

Mom

Tears cascaded down Robert's cheeks. "Sarah, I am so sorry for hurting you," he said, covering his eyes and brushing away the tears. "Sarah, my skin is white, but my soul is black. I had privileges granted me because of the color of my skin, but my soul and my skin color have always been in a battle. I felt Mama knew what was best for me. I have had privileges but not the freedom to be who I am."

Sarah wiped her tears. "I understand. It doesn't erase my anger and pain, but I understand."

Robert extended his hand to his sister. Rose's head slumped forward. Sarah and Robert locked eyes. Sarah slid off her chair to her knees. She buried her face in her mother's lap and clutched Robert's hands. Together, they wrapped their arms around their mother, weeping.

CHAPTER FIFTY-SEVEN

Sarah

Death, like a thief in the night, had silently entered the conference room at Greener Pastures and wrapped his icy-cold fingers around Rose's heart while simultaneously sucking oxygen from her lungs.

Shortly after Sarah got home, Mrs. Jefferson, the director at Greener Pastures called. She told Sarah she needed to meet with her at Greener Pastures at ten o'clock the following morning.

Sleep eluded Sarah as an internal battle raged within her. Her thoughts fought for dominance in her mind. *It wasn't fair!* She could hear the thought screaming in her head. *How many times should I have to deal with death for my mom? Alzheimer's had already killed the mother I knew. Maybe I could have helped her if I had been more vigilant. But no! I was too busy arguing with Robert. She asked us to stop fussing. If I had listened to her, she might still be alive. I might have seen something that would have let me know she needed help.* She was angry with herself. Sarah sat in bed, grabbed her pillow, buried her face, and screamed. Then she used the pillowcase to wipe her tears.

She swung her legs out of bed, sat on the side, and hugged the pillow tightly to her chest. She heard a haunting cry of anguish. She realized it had escaped from the bowels of her spirit. Squeezing the pillow, Sarah rocked back and forth as tears ran like rivers down her face again. The thought that had been trying to fight its way to the front of her consciousness was finally victorious. It came in a raging series of questions. *Why am I angry with Robert? Was it because he left without letting me know? Was it because he passed for white? Was it because he didn't trust me, or was it because I was jealous because I couldn't pass for white?* That last question brought back memories Sarah had hidden away in the crevices of her memory.

She had prayed to God to be like her brother. She wanted white skin and good hair like Robert's when they were in high school; after all, they were twins. She remembered going to People's Drug Store looking for something to bleach her skin, so she bought Nadinola and hid it in her room. She used it every night, getting up the next morning, looking in the mirror, and hoping her skin would be lighter.

A sudden wave of anger hit her. She threw the pillow across the bed. The clock showed two thirty. She paced back and forth across her bedroom floor between her bed and the bedroom door. The more she walked, the more she cried. She finally stopped in the middle of the floor. In about seven hours, she had to meet with Mrs. Jefferson, so she wiped her eyes and nose with the back side of her hand. She wanted to sleep, but instead, she called James to let him know her mother, his sister, was dead.

CHAPTER FIFTY-EIGHT

Sarah and Robert

The next day, in the community room of Greener Pastures, it was quiet but not silent. Emily and Denise sat together at a table. When Janie Ruth entered, she sat alone. Emily and Denise nodded at her, and Janie Ruth tried to muster a fake smile for them. Another roommate was gone. Janie Ruth liked Rose. Her sadness was not so much because of Rose's death—death was a part of being at Greener Pastures, where the smell of death constantly hung in the air, mixing with the smell of disinfectants. Janie Ruth was sad because Rose did not get to spend time with Sidney. She had been so excited for Rose and Sidney.

When Robert walked into the community room, the quietness became silence. Every head turned, and every eye followed him as he walked toward Janie Ruth.

Janie Ruth glanced around the room at all the eyes focused on Robert. She had told him he would need a friend, and now she would be the friend he needed. "Good morning. Please sit down."

Robert could feel eyes on him. By now, he was certain everyone knew he wasn't white, and his name wasn't Richard Fallon. Despite the stares, he was determined to walk in his own truth. He pulled out a chair and sat down, returning Janie Ruth's greeting with a voice that conveyed the pain in his heart. "Good morning," he said.

She reached across the table. She placed her hand on top of Robert's hand. "I'm so sorry about Rose."

He gave her a faint smile. "Thank you. Thank you for caring about her and for not turning your back on me."

"Are you alright?"

"I'm good."

Janie Ruth moved her hand from atop Robert's hand. "Are you sure?"

"Yes, really, I am. Mom's death was bittersweet for me." He wiped the moisture from his eyes. "It was sweet because I got to connect with her." Robert's words choked him. He swallowed hard. "She thought I was still in high school, but she knew who I was." His words again were caught in his throat. He could feel his head starting to ache. He was trying hard not to cry. "My mother knew me. Through Alzheimer's and the absent years, she knew me. For a moment, my mother…." Robert hesitated to try to gain some composure. "The bitter part is she died on my shoulder, and I didn't have a chance to say goodbye because I was too busy arguing with Sarah. Mom had asked us not to argue but to love one another, but Janie Ruth, I know she was happy. She thought I was Sidney because she called me Charlie."

Janie Ruth was relieved that Rose believed she was with Sidney, but her heart ached for Robert. The only solace she could provide was to be a supportive listener. "Robert, I understand there's nothing I can say or do to ease your pain. I know you'll be leaving soon, but please remember that I'm here if you ever need someone to talk to."

Robert dropped his head for a moment. He had only known Janie Ruth since being at Greener Pastures, and she was a closer friend than any friendships he had established since leaving Lynchburg. The bond he felt with her was different. It felt honest. It felt good. He raised his head to speak. He realized his head was no longer aching. "I appreciate...."

Just as Robert was about to tell Janie Ruth how much he appreciated her friendship, the quietness dissipated. Coughs and grunts could be heard at different tables and from corners around the community room. Robert and Janie Ruth turned their heads simultaneously toward the community room entrance and saw Sarah walking toward them. Robert felt tension moving from the top of his head down his body. His heart was pounding like a prisoner beating on prison bars, trying to get out. He did not know what to expect. He did not want a repeat of last night. When Sarah reached their table, Robert stood up to greet her.

"Good morning, Sarah."

Sarah was heavyhearted, but she greeted him with open arms. "Good morning."

Robert walked into his sister's arms and melted in her embrace. A swelling of applause, laughter, and cheers vibrated throughout the community room. He whispered in her ear, "Thank you so much."

She gently tightened her embrace in response to her brother. She whispered back, "I don't want to fight." She then let her hands slide down her brother's arms and into his hands. Sarah turned to Janie Ruth and reached for her hand. She cupped Janie Ruth's hand in her own. "Hi, Miss Janie Ruth."

"Hi. I am so sorry about Rose." Janie Ruth gave a heartbreaking smile.

Sarah, controlled like her mother, responded, "Thank you. I want to thank you for being so kind to my mother."

"Your mama was a special lady. I'm going to miss her."

"My Mom has been my life. I don't know what I am going to do now."

Janie Ruth choked with sorrow. "Time will take care of you."

With a pained smile, Sarah agreed with Janie Ruth. "I know it will." Sarah turned to Robert, still standing beside her, "I need to talk with you." She turned to Janie Ruth, "Would you please give me a few minutes with Robert?"

"Yes, yes!" Janie Ruth pushed her chair from the table.

Robert immediately stepped behind Janie Ruth's chair to assist her. She placed her hands flat on the table to support herself as she rose from her chair.

"Robert, I'll talk with you later." Janie Ruth joined Emily and Denise at their table.

"Please have a seat." Robert pulled out a chair for Sarah. "Are you here to collect Mom's belongings?"

"No, Mrs. Jefferson called me after I left here last night. She asked me to come today. She said she had something to give me. I am to meet her here at ten o'clock this morning." Sarah looked around the community room. "This room holds so many memories." Sarah fought back the tears welling in her eyes. "I guess I could gather Mom's things while I'm here."

Robert pulled a handkerchief from the back pocket of his trousers. He handed it to Sarah. "If you don't mind, I want to help you."

Before Sarah could respond, Mrs. Jefferson entered the community room. Mrs. Jefferson was usually a lively and cheery woman, but today, she appeared a bit melancholy but still walked with purpose. She had a brown envelope in her hand.

Robert stood as she approached their table.

"Good morning, Sarah and Richard. I mean Robert. Robert, please sit."

Robert lowered himself back into his chair.

Mrs. Jefferson did not sit. She sighed, because there was nothing she could say or do to relieve Sarah and Robert's pain, so she gave the customary words of condolence, "I'm so sorry for your loss. Rose was such a beautiful spirit. We are going to miss her here at Greener Pastures."

Sarah and Robert responded simultaneously with good morning and thank you.

Mrs. Jefferson looked at Sarah and said, "Sarah, a week after your mother arrived here, she brought this sealed envelope to me. She asked me to keep it and to give it to you after her death." Mrs. Jefferson handed Sarah the sealed envelope. "If you want privacy, you can use the conference room."

Sarah looked around the community room. She noticed almost every eye in the room was still focused on their table. For some reason, she was not bothered by the attention. She equated the focused eyes not to nosiness but to care for her because of their love for her mom. "Thank you, but I want to stay here if you don't mind. I can feel Mom in here."

Mrs. Jefferson searched Sarah's face. She wasn't sure of what she expected to see. "Are you sure you wouldn't like some privacy? You don't know what is in that envelope."

Sarah smiled, "I'll be alright."

Robert stood, "Mrs. Jefferson, I'm here for her."

"You know we all loved Rose. Please let me know if there is anything I can do."

Sarah smiled. "You are so kind. Thank you."

Mrs. Jefferson hugged Sarah. Robert stood, and Mrs. Jefferson hugged him before leaving. Sarah and Robert sat down. Sarah looked at Robert and placed the envelope on the table. She ran her right hand across its smooth surface, picked it up, and slowly opened it. Inside, she found a white business envelope. She carefully removed and opened it, revealing a letter with a scribbled note taped in the middle of the first page.

Robert searched his sister's face as she silently read the letter.

Dear Sarah,

If you're reading this, it is because I'm no longer with you. I decided to write this letter the day I knew I would be living at Greener Pastures. I know I'm dealing with Alzheimer's and that is scary. I know and understand there might come a time when I will not know who you are. That horrifies me. I can't imagine you standing in front of me and me not recognizing the beautiful child I carried for nine months and gave birth to. The beautiful daughter who has cared for me. Thinking about it makes my heart hurt. Please know no matter what happens, buried deep inside of my soul there is a love for you this disease cannot destroy. If I shall die without telling you I love and appreciate you, please know I love you and appreciate you more than words can express.

Sarah, remember one day you asked me if I would have been accepted in a white neighborhood, living with your father, the way he was accepted in our neighborhood? Remember I told you no. I said I probably would have been killed. Well, I think that is what happened to your father. He was killed because he loved me.

Sarah's eyes widened. "Oh, God!"

"Sarah, what is it?"

Sarah whispered, "Robert, Daddy's death might not have been an accident."

Confused, Robert said, "I don't understand."

"Come sit next to me. Let's read this together."

Robert got up and sat in the chair next to Sarah.

Sarah pointed to the second paragraph of the letter. "Start reading here."

Robert read the paragraph, and he looked up at Sarah. He placed the letter on the table in front of them. Sarah picked it up and held it so they both could see it.

> *Your father owned houses in our neighborhood, but I don't think he was ever welcomed there. One day I was in the hallway at Aunt Rachael's, and I heard a man saying to Aunt Rachael, "We smile saying 'yes sir'. They take our jobs. We say, 'Yes sir'. They sleep with our women. We say, 'Yes sir'. They own houses in our neighborhood, so they think they own us. And we say, 'Yes sir'. Tell her to stay out of*

the line of fire." The words were burned in my memory. I never told anyone what I had heard. I am so sorry I didn't. Taped below is a message your father received. He never told me about it. He gave it to Attorney Berg in a sealed envelope. Attorney Berg gave it to me at the reading of your father's will. Your father said he wanted me to be aware of my surroundings and he wanted me to keep you and your brother safe.

You not wanted here! You take our jobs. You take our women right in our faces. You want to keep living? Go back to your own neighborhood or die. This is not a threat but a promise!

    Sarah's hands started trembling. She laid the letter on the table and turned to Robert. "Why didn't they say something? Why did she leave this note for me?"

    "I don't know. I don't know. Maybe she will tell you in the letter. Do you want to finish reading it here?"

"Yes, I do." Sarah steadied her hands and picked up the letter. They continued reading the letter silently.

> *Now, that I have said that I need to tell you something and I need for you to have an open mind and an open heart. Please don't be angry with me. The truth is your brother left and crossed the color line because I told him to do it. If your father was killed for loving me, I couldn't take a chance on something bad happening to Robert. When the two of you were born, I vowed I would do whatever was necessary to assure your success in life.*

Sarah turned to Robert. They saw the tears welling in each other's eyes. The tears brimming in Sarah's eyes rolled down her face. "Please forgive me for not believing you."

Robert wiped Sarah's tears with his hand. "There is nothing to forgive. Let's finish reading what Mom wrote."

Sarah nodded and held the letter so they could continue reading it.

> *I wanted him to have opportunities that would not be open to him as a colored*

man. Please know he never turned his back on us. Even though he knew your father had made sure we were alright financially, when your brother wrote to me, he put $200.00 in every letter he sent. I didn't tell you this because I felt it would hurt you and I didn't think you would understand. It is hard being colored. It is extremely hard being a colored man. I love both of you so much and I wanted each of you to have the best that life could offer you. I hope you understand what I am trying to say.

    Now, I am asking you to please contact him to let him know about my passing. You will find a telephone number and address for him in the back of my Bible. He is using Richard Fallon as his name. Now, I need you not to be angry with him if he can't attend my service.

You will also find contact information for Attorney Berg. The nursing home also has his contact information. Because they have it, his office will probably contact you, but you can go ahead and call him. He has my will.

Now, you know how you were constantly on me about buying a new mattress because my mattress is so lumpy; and how I constantly told you no? You remember I made you promise not to touch anything in my room until I was no longer on this earth with you? Well, my mattress has all the letters and money your brother sent stuffed in it. All those letters are now yours. I am hoping now *that you know the truth, you will forgive me.*

Please tell your brother I love him with all that I have within me.

Know I am smiling because I am now with my Charlie. Your father and I will always be with you. Whenever you need me, look towards the heavens, or go outside and stand beneath the pear tree and your father and I will be there. We will hear your heart.

Don't be sad. I now have a new mind, a new body, and a new home.

I Love you so very, very much!

Mom

Sarah placed her head on her brother's shoulder as Rose had done. He kissed his twin sister on the top of her head and said, "Come on, twin, let's go gather Mom's things."

As Sarah and Robert exited the community room, they overheard Janie Ruth asking Denise if she would be playing bingo. Denise enthusiastically replied that she was hooked and no longer a bingo virgin. Emily was trying to catch up on the conversation, asking everyone what they were talking about, while Lillie was energetically shouting, "Cigars, cigarettes, Tiparillos!"

Rose's Recipes

Rose cooked with love. She did not measure her ingredients. She eyeballed her ingredients.

Rose's Apple Cobbler

Ingredients:

10 peeled and sliced Granny Smith Apples

2 cups of sugar

1 tablespoon of cinnamon

½ tablespoon of nutmeg

1 teaspoon of vanilla extract

1 teaspoon of lemon extract

1 tablespoon of flour or cornstarch

1 stick of butter – cubed

Crust Ingredients:

2 cups of all-purpose flour

½ teaspoon salt

Very cold water

2 heaping tablespoons of shortening (Crisco) or lard

½ stick of butter – cubed

Directions:

1. Preheat oven to 350 degrees. In a large bowl combine flour and shortening until crumbly. Add in a tablespoon of very cold water and mix. Add small amounts of water as needed until the dough forms a ball. Refrigerate until needed.
2. In a large bowl toss apples with sugar, cinnamon, nutmeg, flour, vanilla, and lemon extract.
3. On a lightly floured surface, roll out dough to about ¼ thickness. Place rolled-out dough in a baking dish. The dough will hang over the edges of the baking dish. Pour the apples into the baking dish. Place a cubed stick of butter over the top of the apples. Fold the top of the apples with the dough. Pierce the top crust and place ½ stick of cubed butter on top of the crust. Bake until apples are tender, and the crust is golden brown, 45 to 55 minutes.

Rose's Corn Pudding

Ingredients:

2 cans of cream corn

1 can of whole grain corn

1 cup of sugar

4 eggs (beaten)

1 teaspoon of vanilla extract

1 teaspoon of lemon strict

½ cup of milk

¾ stick of butter

Directions:

1. Preheat oven to 325 degrees.
2. Combine the milk, flour, and sugar thoroughly. Add corn, butter, vanilla extract, lemon extract, and butter. Mix well. Then add eggs. Mix well.
3. Pour mixture into a baking dish. Bake until firm – 30-45 minutes.

Rose's Sweet Potato Pie

Ingredients:

3 large sweet potatoes

1 ½ cups of sugar

4 eggs

1 can evaporated milk

1 cup butter

1 teaspoon vanilla extract

½ teaspoon lemon extract

½ teaspoon ground nutmeg

½ teaspoon ground cinnamon

2 unbaked pie crust

Directions:

1. Place sweet potatoes in a large pot and cover with water; bring to a boil. Cook until the sweet potatoes are tender. Drain water, peel sweet potatoes, and mash in a bowl. Preheat oven to 425 degrees.
2. Mix butter and eggs together in a bowl until smooth. Stir in mashed sweet potatoes. Mix milk, sugar, vanilla extract, lemon extract, nutmeg, and

cinnamon into the sweet potato mixture. Pour into pie crust.
3. Bake for 40 minutes or until a toothpick inserted in the center of the pie comes out clean. Cool before refrigerating.

Acknowledgments

My first debt of thanks is to my mother, Clytie Rosser Lipford, who transitioned on September 28, 2023. I am who I am because of the sacrifices my mother made. There are stories from my mother sprinkled through *A Mother's White Lie*. Also, Rose's recipes, found at the end of the book are my mom's recipes.

When I was a little girl, my grandmother, Donna Jennings Lipford, corrected the letters I wrote to her with a red pen. She sent those letters back to me with her response to my letters. I did not appreciate it when she did this, but later I did.

My first remembrance of a real interest in writing was sparked by my English teacher, Mrs. Alma Jordan, at Paul Laurence Dunbar High School in Lynchburg, Virginia.

Even though my mother, my grandmother, and my English teacher have passed, I believe if you and I say their names, they will continue to live.

A Mother's White Lie was written because of my daughter Kisha Petticolas and Dorie Smiley. This novel started as a play entitled *Greener Pastures.* When I told Kisha about the play I had written, she said, "Mama, a play is not going to do that story justice. That sounds like a book." I said, "I don't write books; I write plays."

Then, one day I was at the Academy Center of the Arts to talk with Dorie about renting the venue for a production. When I was about to leave, I told her I would probably return because I had written another play. I told her what *Greener*

Pastures was about, and she said, "That sounds like it should be a book." I laughed and left.

Almost a year after hearing Kisha and Dorie say *Greener Pastures* sounded like a book, I decided to take on the challenge. I discovered writing a book was not going to be an easy task. I started writing. I stopped writing. I put my writing on the shelf. I took it off the shelf. This went on for more than five years. I tried to motivate myself by asking Gloria Preston to read chapters as I wrote them. She was diligent, but I stopped and put it on the shelf again.

Then in 2021, my grandson, Joshua Clemons, wrote a story that I helped him get published as a children's book. After that, I looked at myself in the mirror and said, "Shame on you! Your grandson has done something you have been trying to do for five years. Get it together girl!" I took *Greener Pastures* off the shelf again and gave it a new name, *A Mother's White Lie*. This time I completed the writing. Thank you, Joshua, for being my motivation.

Research was an integral part of writing. Thank you, Ted Delany for responding when I asked for information about the Hotel Manhattan. Since I have mentioned research, I must thank my freshman English professor, Mrs. Heath, at Livingstone College. My first research paper, in undergraduate school, was about interracial relationships. The inspiration for this story comes from years of reading and listening to stories from family, friends, and strangers. I was also intrigued by an article I read about a couple, suffering from dementia, having sex in a nursing home.

Before I thank anyone else by name, I need to express my appreciation to people who have had conversations with me knowing you might see what you said in writing or on stage.

I also thank all the people whose conversations I have eased dropped on. You have provided me with a wealth of materials.

Tammy Barnes, at Promedica Hospice in Raliegh, North Carolina, thank you for sharing some general characteristics of Alzheimer's and Dementia. I also thank you for being my mother's hospice nurse. You are a beautiful soul, and you made my mother smile.

The next people I am indebted to are my sister, Angeria Davis, my brother-in-law, Ronnie Davis, and my brother Beverly Lipford, Jr. Angeria, Ronnie, and Beverly, Jr., thank you for sharing your memories of Fifth Street and The Old City Cemetery.

Judy Harvey, at Old City Cemetery, thank you for all your help. I loved your energy, enthusiasm, and eagerness to help. Judy, I called you by name but everyone there was wonderful.

My daughter, Tameka Clemons, thank you for reading the chapter I sent you, and letting me know you wanted to read the next chapter.

Gloria Robinson Simon, Patricia Stokes Worsham, Ted Delaney, and Betsy Garrard, I cannot thank you enough. Gloria, you were the first person to read *A Mother's White Lie*. When you called me to say you could relate to Rose and because of that, you could not read the ending before going to sleep, I did a happy dance when I hung up the telephone. Thank you!

Patty, when you told me you laughed out loud and that Margaret was a bitch, I felt giddy. Patty, I appreciate that you made me dig deeper. You were also kind enough to edit and do a second reading. My heart is full. Thank you!

Ted Delaney, thank you! You took the time to read my manuscript, edit it, and discuss your markings with me. When I left my meeting with you, I said, "Wow!"

Betsy, thank you for volunteering to read and edit my manuscript. When taking on something new or different, there is sometimes a feeling of doubt, a feeling of not being good enough, a feeling of not being worthy. Betsy, after your verbal critiques, I felt like a writer. Your critiques made me feel like I had written something worth reading and discussing. Thank you!

Thanks to all who read this book for your love and support.

About the Author

Jennifer Lipford Petticolas, a retired educator, is a native of Lynchburg, Virginia.

She graduated from Paul Laurence Dunbar High School in Lynchburg. She completed her undergraduate work at Livingstone College in Salisbury, North Carolina.

She earned a Master of English Education and a Master of Educational Leadership from Lynchburg College (University of Lynchburg). Jennifer enjoys writing and directing plays. *A Mother's White Lie* is her debut novel.

www.ingramcontent.com/pod-product-compliance
Lightning Source LLC
LaVergne TN
LVHW061540070526
838199LV00077B/6849